I Actually Did It!

Stephen Shainbart Ph.D.

KEELER PRESS

Published with the help of Indie Authors World
www.indieauthorsworld.com

IndieAuthors
World

This book is dedicated to the two J's of my life: My grandfather Jules, who more than anyone else, showed me that I should have a good life, and to my son Jordan (who is named after Jules), who truly deserves to be dearly loved.

Acknowledgements

I wish to thank the many people helped me with this book: Ian Kerner, my good friend and very bright best-selling author who read an early draft of my book and encouraged me onward, and who then introduced me to my main editor, Emily Blair; Emily Blair who was simply wonderful because her feedback was brilliant, insightful, and encouraging at the same time; Rachel Ince, who also read an early draft and supported me; Dr. Randy Katz, for hiring me as a psychologist and making it possible for me to become Canadian; Kim Macleod, owner of my publishing company Indie Authors World, for her super competence and warm supportive character; to Larry Glickman, Cornell University history professor and my dear friend from high school - I am so grateful to have had such an intelligent and kind man help me with my book and also throughout my life; my cousin/friend Rob who also was among the first to read it and gave me thoughtful and valuable feedback; my sister Cindy for also reading early drafts of the book and her perceptive observations, and also for not dying from the coronavirus after her hospitalization.

Contents

1
Introduction

"There's no way Trump is going to win."

"The Mueller Report will get him. So don't worry."

"He's going to be impeached and removed from office."

"He's going to be a one-term president and he will be gone in four years. And then everything will go back to normal."

When I started to write this book, it was December 2019. At that point, the first two statements above were already disproved, and now the third one is as well. The last one, that Trump will be gone in 2020, is far from assured.

It seemed to me that a lot of people in my New York City bubble in 2016 were using wishful thinking as a defense mechanism in order to cope with the scary thought Donald Trump could be elected president of the United States. And they continued to use wishful thinking to defend themselves from the distinct possibility he would complete his term and could be re-elected.

Wishful thinking has never been my way of coping with anxiety. For example, in the 1990s I took a yoga class. At the end of the class the teacher dimmed the lights and told everyone to sit and close their eyes, relax, and imagine that they were at a beautiful and tranquil lake. He then instructed us to silently repeat to ourselves, "I have no worries, I have no worries, I have no worries." I looked around at the class and everyone seemed so relaxed, all breathing slowly with their eyes closed. However, I very clearly remember thinking, "What the hell is he talking about? I have plenty of worries. I don't know if I'm going to be able to get enough subjects to complete my dissertation, and if I can't do that, all the work all these months I've done on it is going to be wasted."

And then I began thinking about all my other worries. Was my girlfriend at the time going to be in a bad mood again because I didn't spend enough time with her because I was too focused on my dissertation? And so on.

Next, I told myself, "Anyway, I'm not at a tranquil lake: I'm on a third-floor walk-up in Chelsea in Manhattan. Are things really so bad I have to tell myself lies to deal with reality?"

I'm telling you this story because I think it has something to do with the fact that while many people entertained the thought of moving to Canada because of Trump, I'm one of the very few that actually did it. In fact, on the night of the 2016 election, the Canadian immigration website crashed because it was flooded with so many Americans researching the possibility of emigrating to Canada. But, of all those people, statistics show only a tiny number followed through on it.[1]

This book is the story of someone that moved to Canada in response to Donald Trump becoming the president of the United States. I wrote it because I thought it might be illuminating to the millions of Americans who thought about doing the Canada thing, but then went on with their lives at home.

I know bad things can and do happen, and I don't escape them by imagining tranquil lakes. I feel better knowing bad things can be faced and resolved somehow. And my way of resolving the problem known as Trump was to become a dual citizen of the USA and Canada. In November 2019, I became a permanent resident of Canada. As a permanent resident, I can now do all the things any Canadian citizen

1 - https://www.businessinsider.com/trump-win-americans-not-moving-to-canada-2017-7

can do, except vote or hold a national security job. I'm in; I actually did it. I even recently received my government healthcare card. And I still retain my American citizenship.

I'm a psychologist. One of my patients, whom I've been working with for many years and knows me well, said to me I'll turn out to either be a genius or an idiot. We'll see if either of those turns out to be true.

My whole journey since the 2016 election to become Canadian was incredibly hard. The truth is that it was much more difficult than I'd ever imagined. In all honesty, I'm not sure I'd do it again if I'd known how hard it was going to be for me. I mean that: I'm really not sure. And for three years I lived in a constant state of anxiety that I'd fail – that all my efforts and sacrifices would amount to nothing. But at least it's over now, and I was successful. I'm proud of myself. It's a good feeling.

In this book, I'll describe what I went through. Not only was much of it arduous, but some of it was ridiculous. At moments, downright bizarre.

A Note on Relativity

After telling Canadians my stories, opinions, experiences, and impressions of Canada, I've come to notice an important variable in their responses to them. This variable is relativity. When I'm relating such opinions, and impressions, etc., of Canada to Canadians, I've noticed they don't always agree with my descriptions of their country. But please try to understand that this book is written from the perspective of a New Yorker. It may not match your experience, because perceptions are relative.

There are many examples of this relativity. Here's just one illustration. For example, Torontonians believe Toronto rents are very expensive. And, from their perspective, they're right. Toronto is more expensive than almost anywhere in Canada, except Vancouver. And moreover, in the last five years, their rents have skyrocketed. Toronto rents are very, very high.

But Toronto rents are not high compared with New York City. Rents in Toronto are less than half of the rents in New York.[2] My landlord was asking about $1,200 (USD) a month for my one-bedroom apartment in the heart of downtown Toronto with a large, private outdoor deck, with a washer and dryer in the unit. Any New Yorker would be shocked at how low this is. I just looked up the average rent of a one-bedroom apartment in Manhattan, and it's in the neighborhood of $3,500 (USD). Get my point?

From what they tell me, Canadians outside Toronto often have a stereotype of Torontonians as cold-hearted city people. Many find Toronto to be too crowded, too urban, and overstimulating. Relative to the rest of Canada, Toronto is an urban jungle.

However, after visiting Toronto, my 15-year-old son, who is from Brooklyn, said in all seriousness, "I like Toronto. It's so peaceful and relaxing. It's like going away to the country."

One more example of relativity. In 2017 I visited China and spent some time in a city called Chongqing. The city of Chongqing has about 30 million people. The entire nation of Canada has 37 million people. The population of Toronto is less than three million. New York City has less than nine million people.

Times Square in Manhattan is one of the most crowded places in New York City. Walking around Chongqing felt like being in Times Square at peak hour. Except that in Chongqing, throughout the city, it felt like Times Square all the time, day or night.

In Chongqing, people in their 40s told me they'd not seen the sky be blue since they were children, because of pollution. Anyone, not just tourists, who drinks water from the kitchen tap in Chongqing will get very sick. Because of the pollution, all people must boil the water before drinking it. Hell, even in the Beijing airport, the water fountains had machines to boil the water first.

---

2 - https://www.numbeo.com/cost-of-living/compare_cities.
jsp?country1=Canada&city1=Toronto&country2=United+States&city2=New+York%2C+NY

When I got back to New York City from China, I felt like I'd gone back to a goddamned national park. I'm so grateful I went to China, because I've come to appreciate New York, and many other places, in ways I never could have done before. So, just as New York can feel like a relaxing, uncrowded, and unpolluted place compared with Chongqing, Toronto can feel like a quiet, soothing town to a New Yorker. Everything is relative.

I'm not only talking about crowdedness. I'm making the larger point that I'll perceive the cultural norms in Toronto and Canada differently than a native would, and what strikes me may not match your experience. In other words, I'm saying that how one perceives a place is always based on one's vantage point. Therefore, I'm urging you to try to understand that if my experiences don't match yours, and even if you feel offended, to consider that everything is relative to where I'm coming from.

Another quick point I want to make is that I lived my entire life in New York City and then moved to Toronto. New York City and Toronto are both international cities, and by far the largest metropolises in their counties, and also not typical of their countries. Many people in the United States regard New York as practically not part of their United States, and the same with Canadians about Toronto not really being part of Canada. I honestly don't know what it's like to live in rural Manitoba, Wyoming, or Alabama, etc. So if you're from a place that's the antithesis of a major city, my perspective may be completely different from yours as well, regardless of what country you come from.

So please remember this book may or may not resonate with your sensibilities, and I hope that's okay with you. I mean, as Mark Twain put it, it's the differences of opinion that makes horse races. Perspectives can be broadened. Actually, isn't that the point of traveling to different places? In fact, traveling to different places to gain different perspectives is what this book is all about.

2

To Justify Myself in the Independent Stand I Was Compelled to Take

(Or, "Why the Hell Did I Do this?") - Part One

"To Justify Myself in the Independent Stand I was Compelled to Take" comes from a quote by Thomas Jefferson (I don't mean to brag, but I came up with the "Why the hell did I do this?" part). Ironically, I'm drawing from Thomas Jefferson to explain why I left the United States. Jefferson said his purpose in writing America's Declaration of Independence was:

> *"Not to find out new principles or new arguments never before thought of. Not merely to say things which were never said before. But to place before mankind the common sense of the subject, in terms so plain and firm, as to command their assent; and to justify ourselves in the independent stand we are compelled to take."*[3]

What a gorgeous writer he was. They picked the right guy to write the Declaration.

My reasons for becoming Canadian and leaving the United States aren't original. Millions of Americans share my views and feelings about Donald Trump and what's going on in the USA. But Jefferson was implying in the quote above that originality isn't always important.

3 - 3 - https://www.loc.gov/exhibits/jefferson/jeffleg.html#:~:text=not%20to%20find%20out%20new,independent%20stand%20we%20%20%5Bwere%5D%20compelled

Sometimes it's more important to explain yourself clearly to others than it is to come up with a completely new idea. This is why I wrote this book: to explain why I felt I was compelled to leave the United States and move to Canada. I also wrote it to describe what that process was like for me.

Let me make something very clear. I love the founding principles of the United States. No, not the hypocritical shit, like slavery and the genocide of the native Americans, which is horrible beyond words (while slavery was never big in Canada, it does share with the United States a horrific history of genocide of their indigenous peoples). I mean that I love the good stuff about the USA, such as its core principles. And sometimes Americans actually followed these principles. I remain proud to be American and I'm proud of the foundation of the United States.

For more than two years now I've heard many Canadians convey a certain smugness about not being American. For example, one of my clients told me, "The United States is the only Third World country with running water" (okay, that's funny). Another client half-jokingly (and half-seriously) expects me to walk around with a gun as a way to settle disputes. Yeah, sure, just like every other Jewish psychologist in Manhattan. The truth is, other than police officers or soldiers, I've only seen a person carry a gun once in my life.

When I talk about the amazing founding principles of the United States, Canadians often respond with some version of "I didn't know that." I wish more Canadians knew about this history before forming their stereotypes of the United States.

In 18th-Century Europe, while the Enlightenment philosophers were debating how people could govern themselves, the European people (and Canadians) were still being ruled by kings and queens. The United States went ahead by itself, threw off the monarchs, and restored democracy to the world. Democratic government on any significant scale had been missing from the earth for more than a thousand years, ever since the ancient Roman Republic fell. Because of this, the United States of America is a great accomplishment.

The United States was also the first colony in the history of the world to successfully become independent from its mother country. Not only that, but moreover Americans took on the most powerful kingdom in the world, Great Britain, and won. We built our own country, from the ground up. We designed our own system of government on very sound principles, based on the lessons of history. When you really think about it, all of these are incredible achievements.

Canada, by contrast, didn't become its own country until 1867, and it largely imported the British model of government. It gradually and incrementally negotiated its freedom over like ... a century. A century in which the USA had already achieved its freedom. Yes, Canadian independence was peaceful, and not spilling blood and avoiding violence is a very good thing. But my blood is American, and I'm very proud of what my people accomplished. Some things were worth fighting for, and American independence was one of them.

I am not a historian and I hope I don't bore you with history. I just want to describe this in a bit more detail, because I want to explain what makes America great to me. This is important because it's part of the reason I'm so disturbed about what is happening in my country now. And it also explains why I'm so distressed about anyone who tries to destroy these things, because they are anti-American, in my view. I'm explaining all this a bit more because it's how I'm going to make my case for why Trump and his supporters, while believing they are patriots, are actually anti-American. I believe it's important to protect and defend American values from these people.

I've read the many letters Thomas Jefferson and John Adams wrote to each other over many decades. Both were, of course, Founding Fathers, and presidents, and both were very erudite. Along with the other founders, they studied and analyzed the ancient Greeks and Romans and drew from them in designing the United States. Their letters are full of references to the works of the ancients. They drew on their knowledge of many books about history, learning the lessons of past civilizations, to create the first modern democracy in the world.

They studied and analyzed why the ancient Roman Republic, which was a democracy, fell and became a dictatorship. The founders tried to design a system of government that would prevent this from happening in the new American Republic. They learned lessons from the past in creating a republic that would endure. For all these things, I have the utmost respect and admiration for them.

Of course, in the beginning democracy was very limited to white males who owned property, hardly democratic by today's standards. But, by the standards of the time, which I think is a fairer comparison, it was extraordinary, because power was no longer limited to the kings and queens. Moreover, because this democratic system came from the Enlightenment, it was able to expand on itself. The Enlightenment, as Todd Gitlin wrote in *The Twilight of Common Dreams*[4], is self-correcting. The original premise of self-government was gradually but greatly expanded to many other groups. Of course, the process is far from perfect and significant injustices remain (the suppressing of votes by Republicans, anyone?), but I'm discussing the breakthrough the United States represented compared with other countries in the 1700s.

I admire the founders for so many things. For example, they created the system of "checks and balances," that power is to be divided between the three branches of government: the President, the Congress, and the Courts. No one branch could become a dictator; each branch could "check" the power of the other branch if necessary. This is all basic high school history.

But Donald Trump and his Administration are whacking away at all of this, repeatedly seeking to damage this important system of checks and balances created by our founders. Of course, it's true that there's been a slow and steady expansion of presidential power almost since the creation of the office, most markedly in recent years under George W. Bush during the "War on Terror." However, the Trump Administration has carried this to new extremes, openly rejecting

---

4 - THE TWILIGHT OF COMMON DREAMS Why America Is Wracked by Culture Wars. By Todd Gitlin. 294 pp. New York: Metropolitan Books/ Henry Holt & Company.

any kind of accountability. Used to his role as head of the Trump Organization, in which he answered to no one, Trump has brought the same autocratic attitude to the presidency.

The most obvious of these abuses has been the Administration's constant, unabashed obstruction of justice. The firing of James Comey, the attempts to intimidate Robert Mueller, and the suppression of the Mueller report became a dress rehearsal for the Administration's behavior during the impeachment proceedings. Efforts to silence the whistle-blower in the Ukraine affair were followed by witness tampering and complete refusal to honor requests for information or subpoenas. As Jerry Nadler pointed out, Nixon provided Congress with dozens of recordings, Clinton gave his blood, but Donald Trump "refused to produce a single document and directed every witness not to testify."[5]

Instead, the Trump Administration has declared "absolute immunity" for close presidential aides, a new doctrine winding its way to the Supreme Court (the court recently rejected another of Trump's broad claims for immunity, saying he couldn't refuse a subpoena for his financial records, so there's reason to hope).

Not only does the Trump Administration refuse to answer to Congress' legal oversight, but it has also disregarded Congress' control of appropriations. Along with the ensuing obstruction of justice, it was Trump's withholding of Senate-approved aid to Ukraine for his own political gain that formed the basis of his impeachment. Perhaps even more outrageously, Trump diverted money Congress had allocated to the military to his misguided wall project, claiming he could use his emergency powers to do so. This case, too, is making its way through the courts – most recently, the 9th US Circuit Court of Appeals said the White House didn't have the constitutional authority to re-appropriate funds Congress had denied. Unfortunately, the money had

---

5 - Paz, Christian. "Read Jerry Nadler's Opening Statement in the Judiciary Committee's Impeachment Hearing," *The Atlantic*, December 4, 2019. https://www.theatlantic.com/politics/archive/2019/12/jerry-nadler-impeachment-opening-statement/602983/

already been spent with the blessing of the Supreme Court, to which the Administration will now likely appeal.

Trump's attitude toward this other main branch of the government, the judiciary, is no better. With the Republicans in charge of the Senate, the judiciary has served as one of the most important checks on the Administration's outrages. It's a resistance that has filled Trump with fury. He's famously abused judges, starting during his campaign with claims the judge overseeing the class-action lawsuit against Trump University had a conflict of interest due to his Mexican heritage. He went on to call a judge who ruled against his travel ban a "so-called judge," and his ruling "ridiculous."[6] He attacked another who decided against his policy of rejecting asylum seekers who enter the country illegally, calling him "an Obama judge" and drawing a rare rebuke from Chief Justice Roberts that there's no such thing, but instead that "independent judiciary is something we should all be thankful for."

Trump, of course, was less than thankful, responding that "you do indeed have 'Obama judges' and they have a much different point of view than the people who are charged with the safety of our country."[7] Most recently, Trump unleashed his anger at the Supreme Court for its decision that he doesn't have immunity from subpoenas for his financial records. He made his familiar complaint about a "political prosecution" in the usual series of whining tweets: "Courts in the past have given 'broad deference.' BUT NOT ME!"[8]

6 - Amy Wang, "Trump Lashes out at 'so-Called Judge' Who Temporarily Blocked Travel Ban," *The Washington Post*, February 4, 2017. https://www.washingtonpost.com/news/the-fix/wp/2017/02/04/trump-lashes-out-at-federal-judge-who-temporarily-blocked-travel-ban/

7 - Robert Barnes, "Rebuking Trump's Criticism of 'Obama Judge,' Chief Justice Roberts Defends Judiciary as 'Independent'," *The Washington Post*, November 21, 2018. https://www.washingtonpost.com/politics/rebuking-trumps-criticism-of-obama-judge-chief-justice-roberts-defends-judiciary-as-independent/2018/11/21/6383c7b2-edb7-11e8-96d4-0d23f2aaad09_story.html

8 - John Wagner, "Trump Says He's a Victim of 'Political Prosecution' after Supreme Court Rulings," *The Washington Post*, July 9, 2020. https://www.washingtonpost.com/powerpost/trump-says-hes-victim-of-political-prosecution-after-supreme-court-rulings/2020/07/09/12b49d78-bf81-11ea-b178-bb7b-05b94af1_story.html

The media, though not constitutionally recognized like that of the other two branches of government, is another important check on presidential power, and Trump's relationship with reporters is also abusive. He has refused to answer questions, eliminated regular daily briefings, restricted access to his staff, and tried to remove White House press credentials of critical media. Also, the Justice Department under Trump has harassed journalists with prosecutions to reveal their sources, and Customs has hassled journalists as they crossed borders. The Trump campaign has sued *The New York Times*, *The Washington Post* and CNN for libel.

Some of these strategies were pursued by previous Administrations, but what's unique to the Trump Administration is his unceasingly hostile rhetoric. Trump continually denounces the media as "fake news" and "the enemy of the people," as he literally rallies his followers against them, resulting in threats to reporters. This drumbeat of denigration, along with a limiting of access to government sources, has led to a growing distrust of media.[9]

Nor are there any voices of dissent allowed within his Administration. Like a king, Trump surrounds himself with sycophants who must sing his praises or be fired. His reliance on unofficial agents such as Rudy Giuliani sets the stage for unethical and unaccountable behavior. And his unrelenting fury at Jeff Sessions for recusing himself from the Russia investigation makes it clear he has no regard whatsoever not only for dissent, but for even the semblance of objectivity.

Donald Trump and his followers are trying to dismantle the core foundations of the United States set up by its Founding Fathers, including its critical system of checks and balances. They wish to rid themselves of any accountability, official or unofficial. They're trying to destroy America as we know it.

I've thought of another way that Trump and his supporters are anti-American. I want to add that this is another thing that many

9 - Leonard Downie, "The Trump Administration and the Media," The Committee to Protect Journalists, April 16, 2020. https://cpj.org/reports/2020/04/trump-media-attacks-credibility-leaks/

Canadians seem unaware of when they boast of not being American. The United States is the first country in the history of the world to have no national religion. Jefferson was a big part of that too, by the way. He fought hard to ensure the United States didn't belong to only the Protestants, or the Catholics, or the Jews, or the Hindus, or the Muslims, or anyone else.

Let me ask you a question. Who do you think is currently defending this founding principle? Is it Donald Trump and the Republicans, who have evangelical Christians as their base? Is it the people who want to make America a Christian nation, and therefore destroy this core foundation of the United States? Who are the real patriots who are defending American principles? Is it the flag-waving Republican Trump supporters, or is it the people who vote against Trump and support the separation of church and state?

Question: So if I hold American principles in such high regard, why am I moving to Canada?

Well, I just spoke about how erudite the American founders were, and how they read ancient history and philosophy and drew upon this when creating the United States. And now we have … this person as our president. A man who appears unaware of what exactly the Pearl Harbor attack entailed, pulling then-chief of Staff John Kelly aside while on a tour of the U.S.S. Arizona memorial in Hawaii to ask, "Hey, John, what's this all about? What's this a tour of?" A man who turned to French President Macron during a Bastille Day parade to reveal that he didn't realize until that moment that the French "had won a lot of battles."[10]

In his 2019 Independence Day speech at the Lincoln Memorial, Trump talked about the history of American military victories. About the Revolutionary War, he said: "Our army manned the air, it rammed the ramparts, it took over airports, it did everything it had

---

10 - Philip Rucker and Carol D. Leonnig, A Very Stable Genius: Donald J. Trump's Testing of America. (New York: Penguin Press, 2020), 169-70.

to do and at Fort McHenry, under the rocket's red glare, it had nothing but victory."[11]

Trump talked about the "rocket's red glare" during the Revolutionary War. But in his lyrics to "The Star-Spangled Banner," Francis Scott Key was actually referencing a battle during the War of 1812, some 33 years after the Revolutionary War ended. Confusing two different wars 33 years apart – okay, I would expect no less from Trump.

But a president talking about seizing the airports during the late 1700s or early 1800s? Let me say that again, in case you missed it: Trump actually said the American military seized British airports in the late 1700s or early 1800s.

Remember Canada was part of Great Britain then, whom we fought in both wars in those days. So, now let's fast forward to 2019.

I'm at Billy Bishop airport in Toronto. I'm checking in, getting my boarding pass on Porter Airlines, which is a Canadian airline that flies between New York and Toronto, among other places.

"Where are you going?" the ticket agent asks me.

"New York, I say." I pause. Then I say, "I'm an American. And you should be very grateful to my people. We seized your airports in the 1700s. Maybe even this one. If we weren't so nice as to give it back to you, you wouldn't have this job. You should be grateful."

She smiled with me and replied. "You're absolutely right; I read all about that in the newspaper."

As Harlan Ellison said: "You are not entitled to your opinion. You are entitled to your informed opinion. No one is entitled to be ignorant."[12]

The United States has gone from a country created and governed by very well-read, brilliant thinkers steeped in history, to a moron who never reads and claims airports existed in the 1700s. Even worse, many people chose him because of exactly that – precisely

---

11 - David Jackson, "Donald Trump Trips up on History in 4th of July Speech, Mentions Airports during Revolutionary War," *USA Today*, July 5, 2019. https://www.usatoday.com/story/news/politics/2019/07/04/independence-day-donald-trump-trips-up-revolutionary-war-history/1638531001/

12 - https://www.goodreads.com/quotes/9972-you-are-not-entitled-to-your-opinion-you-are-entitled

because he's not knowledgeable and educated. Personally, I think many Trump supporters gravitate toward him because he serves to elevate their self-esteem. Trump disdains experts and education and can be seen as "really sticking it to the elites." By doing so, he can make his less educated followers feel they have "turned the tables" on those with more education or achievement, which in turn makes them feel better about themselves.

Trump openly relies on a lack of education in his base. As he said after his win in the Nevada primary: "We won the evangelicals. We won with young. We won with old. We won with highly educated. We won with poorly educated. I love the poorly educated."

Trump's particular triumph with what he characterized as "the poorly educated," went on to prove true in the general election. According to Pew exit polling, 43 percent of Clinton voters were college graduates, compared with 29 percent of Trump voters.[13] If we look at white voters only, 67 percent without a college degree voted for Trump, a gap not seen since 1980. It should be noted that white college graduates also voted for Trump, but the gap there was only four percent, similar to the 2008 election.[14] Famed statistician Nate Silver pointed out in his analysis of voters who shifted their vote from one party to the other, "it appears as though educational levels are the critical factor in predicting shifts in the vote between 2012 and 2016," with voters of high school education or less handing Trump the victory.[15]

And yet to be less educated isn't always to be "poorly educated." With his offensive phrasing, Trump indicates another aspect of his

13 - "An Examination of the 2016 Electorate, Based on Validated Voters," Pew Research Center, August 9, 2018. https://www.pewresearch.org/politics/2018/08/09/an-examination-of-the-2016-electorate-based-on-validated-voters/

14 - Alec Tyson and Shiva Maniam, "Behind Trump's Victory: Divisions by Race, Gender and Education," Pew Research Center, November 9, 2016. https://www.pewresearch.org/fact-tank/2016/11/09/behind-trumps-victory-divisions-by-race-gender-education/

15 - Nate Silver, "Education, Not Income, Predicted Who Would Vote For Trump," FiveThirtyEight, November 22, 2016. https://fivethirtyeight.com/features/education-not-income-predicted-who-would-vote-for-trump/

voters – their lack of knowledge about government and disdain for critical thought. Research has shown that "low-information voters," who avoided activities that challenged their thinking abilities or didn't know basic facts about government, strongly preferred Trump. Again, these are white voters, with these qualities also being linked with racist attitudes toward Muslims and African-Americans.[16] Multiple studies have unsurprisingly shown Fox News viewers to be least informed (most recently about the coronavirus).[17]

I believe another major motivation for many Trump supporters, besides the need to maintain self-esteem, is resentment. "Sticking it to the elites," is a perfect way to simultaneously boost self-esteem (by turning the tables on them) while also expressing resentment. It's been widely pointed out that much of white, working-class America has been losing status and, in some ways, economic opportunities in the USA, and many people are angry about that. As a psychologist, I know that anger comes from hurt or a feeling of being threatened. The person may not consciously feel hurt or threatened, and they may go straight to anger in their emotional experience. But anger always emanates from some sense of hurt. Like other animals, people can become angry and fight back when they feel threatened. I think this is what's going on with many Trump supporters. One sign of this hurt is the widespread opioid epidemic among this group. There is pain here.

I think a lot of Trump supporters don't even like Trump that much as a person, but they like that he's a conduit for their anger against the elites that they feel look down on them and are responsible for their

---

16 - Richard Fording and Sanford Schram, "'Low Information Voters' Are a Crucial Part of Trump's Support," The Washington Post, November 7, 2016. https://www.washingtonpost.com/news/monkey-cage/wp/2016/11/07/low-information-voters-are-a-crucial-part-of-trumps-support/ Fording and Schram asked respondents whether they agreed or disagreed that "Thinking is not my idea of fun" and "I would rather do something that requires little thought than something that is sure to challenge my thinking abilities." To test knowledge of government, they asked how long senatorial terms were and which of four policy areas had least government spending.

17 - Christopher Ingraham, "New Research Explores How Conservative Media Misinformation May Have Intensified the Severity of the Pandemic," June 25, 2020. https://www.washingtonpost.com/business/2020/06/25/fox-news-hannity-coronavirus-misinformation/

loss of power and status. And that makes them feel good, and so they vote for him.

They're not entirely wrong. As a New Yorker, I generally see very little sympathy or empathy for the white working-class people in the USA who've lost power or status. Many of my fellow New Yorkers do regard these people as morons whose problems deserve little concern compared with visual minorities: LGBT rights, etc. I'm not arguing whether they deserve more empathy; that's a whole other can of worms. I am saying there's some truth to the way they feel liberal Americans regard them. And, therefore, it's not surprising they resent the "elites" and vote for someone like Trump.

I personally don't see how any of these voters can be persuaded to vote for a Democratic candidate while they are sometimes regarded with contempt. Don't get me wrong: the disregard for science, the relative lack of education, the frequent lack of tolerance for people who vary from the "norm" are all things I abhor about many of these voters. I'm saying, however, that they are people, and their feelings shouldn't be disregarded, and most importantly, you cannot win their votes by having nothing but contempt for them.

You see, in my view I'm not really not leaving the United States. In my opinion, Americans, by voting for Trump, left America. What makes America different are its founding principles, as I just discussed. And these principles are based upon knowledge and an appreciation of history and a desire to learn from history. They are also about having checks and balances. They are about keeping religion out of government. Disregard the importance of knowledge, and these other principles, and you are unAmerican. Full stop. It's the adherence to these principles, based in knowledge, that made America special. Trump and his supporters, by violating these things, are anti-American. While claiming to make America great, they are taking actions to dismantle the very things that actually made America great.

In my view, America is not so much a place as it's an idea. I felt compelled to flee the country because I remain committed to these

American principles. Frankly, I believe they're being practiced in Canada much more than in the current United States. I've moved to a place that's more American than the United States has become, at least in some fundamental respects.

I want to add that I'll never give up my American citizenship. I'll most certainly vote against Trump and I'll work hard in the upcoming election to defeat him, for one purpose: to make America great again.

***

A couple of years ago, I went on a date in NYC with a woman who grew up in Asia but moved to the United States and became an American citizen. Prior to living in NYC, however, she lived in Canada for some time. I remember very clearly what she said to me. She said "Canada does all the stuff America talks about doing – the land of immigrants and accepting all people – but they do it better." That's what I'm saying here.

I mean, just take any American coin out of your pocket and look at it. It says "E Pluribus Unum": Latin for "From Many, One." Trump, through his anti-immigration stance, is trying to take away the "From Many" part.

My friend Bill texted me a couple of years ago, while we were talking about my quest to move to Canada. I saved it.

He wrote: *"In a funny way, it's a completely American story. Because you are an American patriot who moved to maintain his American values and sanity."*

And he added: *"You decided to maintain a divided residence to maintain a whole soul. The point of your story is that it's so ordinary. But you had the guts to do something."*

One last thing, and it's not about history. It's just common sense, and I'm going to write it plainly. I left the USA because I don't want to be in a place that's run by a dick. I also left because I don't want to live in a country where the people actively chose a complete dick to be their leader. Did I write that plainly enough?

That a person such as Trump, who's a serial liar (Forbes magazine reports that Trump has told 23.3 lies per day in 2020)[18], ignorant (using disinfectants to treat the coronavirus), sometimes delusional – Trump said he "watched in Jersey City, N.J., where thousands and thousands of people were cheering" as the World Trade Center was destroyed" (when there's no evidence of it)[19] – capable of such cruelty (e.g., "grab them by the pussy," making fun of handicapped people), and so many other statements, could be chosen by the people to be president is profoundly disturbing. There are jerks in every country, but not every country chooses to elect a jerk. If the people wanted to elect a Republican, that's one thing, but choosing to elect a jerk, regardless of party, is another.

I'm talking about basic human values. This has nothing to do with politics. This has nothing to do with the Republican party or the Democratic party. Donald Trump is a bad human being, and he lives out these bad values. Problematically, enough Americans either liked this or at least were willing to overlook it even though they had other Republican candidates to choose from. To me, that means there's something wrong with America. At the least, it suggests that there's something wrong with many Americans and their values.

Many people have asked me if my moving to Canada will turn out to be pointless, even foolish, if Trump is defeated in the upcoming election. I don't think so, even if I hope that happens. My thinking is that since Americans were able to vote for such a person in 2016, they can vote for a similar (or even worse) person in the future. Because of the poor judgment among too many American voters, there's poor quality control among its people in choosing their leaders. In a decently functioning democracy, such a person should have never been considered a serious candidate for president, let alone successfully elected. Therefore,

18 - https://www.forbes.com/sites/davidmarkowitz/2020/05/05/
trump-is-lying-more-than-ever-just-look-at-the-data/#2a8387661e17
19 - https://www.politifact.com/factchecks/2015/nov/22/donald-trump/
fact-checking-trumps-claim-thousands-new-jersey-ch/

our country is not functioning on a decent (in all senses of the term) level. And that problem will not disappear merely because Trump may lose the next election.

It's disillusioning. It's also scary. That's why I wanted a Plan B, an option outside of the United States, in case the shit really hits the fan. I also felt unhappy, sad inside, about being part of such a place.

As columnist Andrew Coyne so well summed it up in an op-ed in the Canadian newspaper *The Globe and Mail,* "Over the past four years, it has been hard to escape the feeling that much of America – and even some Canadians – had fallen under the spell of a cult."[20] He goes on to discuss how Trump's virulent personality has infected many of his followers, to the detriment of their characters. Trumpism, he says, "represents the triumph of unreason and the suppression of differences. To pay the usual respects to such an unworthy opponent is to do dishonor to one's worthy opponents." He rightly identifies support for Trump as a "moral failing." Well said, Mr. Coyne.

I want to add one other thing. As a New Yorker, I've known about Donald Trump my entire life. Like riding the subway, knowing about Trump has always just been a part of being a New Yorker. I knew about the guy well before he was considered a politician. And I've always thought he was a jerk. Millions of New Yorkers have felt the same way. Trump won 18 percent of the vote in New York City; that means 82 percent of New Yorkers voted against him. And these are the people who know him best.[21]

He would always appear in the gossip columns, on TV shows, anywhere and everywhere he could possibly get attention. I remember reading a newspaper piece that described how he picks his women like a 13-year-old boy would, according to their resemblance to Barbie dolls. I remember one time a man imitating the Russian leader Gorbachev

20 - Andrew Coyne, "Opinion: The Virus of Trumpism and His Infectious Moral Failings," *The Globe and Mail,* February 12, 2020. https://www.theglobeandmail.com/opinion/article-the-virus-of-trumpism-and-his-infectious-moral-failings/

21 - https://www.businessinsider.com/trump-vote-in-new-york-city-staten-island-2016-11

was out and about and Donald Trump came down to the street to meet him and was fooled. Overall, I just remember that Donald Trump always represented the opposite of what I value most in human beings and demonstrated the worst in people. I couldn't stand him, and I tried not to think about him when the media would shove him in my face. When *The Apprentice* was on, I turned the channel. I thought it was all bullshit.

And as a life-long New Yorker, I personally know several people that know or have had interactions with Donald Trump. Some people over the years have told me stories about him well before he ran for president. I'm going to leave them vague to protect people's privacy. But I can say some things. One person met him at a party and had an awful interaction with him, as he was arrogant and dismissive. The person told me about their interaction years ago, well before he ran for president. But I never forgot the story because it was so horrible. Still another person grew up in Queens and knew people in his family and had some pretty interesting things to say about him. One person started a business when he was a young man and did some work for him, and Trump refused to pay him after he finished, and the man almost lost his business. In fact there are many such stories like this from people who Trump hired and then refused to pay them for their services. It's all out there; this was even part of the debate with Hillary.

So what I've heard about him through the grapevine not only confirms what we know publicly about the man, but it indicates he's even worse than the media is telling us.

It all comes down to this, dear reader. I'm not only moving to Canada because Trump and his followers betray American values, although that's a huge part of it. I'm also moving to Canada because Trump and his followers support a bad person. Sometimes I hear that Trump supporters know he's not a good person but they wanted to support their conservative agenda through Trump. I don't buy this rationalization. Conservatives could have voted for another candidate, such as Ted Cruz, or others. Instead, they chose this most dishonest man. Because they chose him, Trump is a mirror image of them.

Similarly, even though I'm aware so many didn't support him (myself included), Americans voted him into office. Therefore the president is also a reflection of who Americans are as a people and as a nation. We the people selected him. He is us. I say screw that.

I choose not to be part of such a place.

Trump's Narcissism

When people ask me why I moved to Canada, I often reply by saying "Because a mentally ill and cruel man took power in my country. And even worse, the people chose him."

That's my brief reply. In the longer version, I elaborate and say that because I believe he's mentally ill and cruel, a serial liar, and lacks qualities like integrity and empathy, will not make decisions that are good for my country, my family, and myself. And such poor decisions may be catastrophic in the short-term and/or in the long-term.

As I write this, Trump's making false claims about the coronavirus. I believe the president's personality is ill-suited to respond to the reality of the virus. He's better suited to respond to the political effects of the virus and how it makes him look. In other words, the virus isn't a Trump supporter or a Trump opposer; it's a thing unto itself, and I doubt whether Trump can respond to any challenge by seeing it for what it is instead of how it will affect him. In fact, at the end of this book I will discuss how Trump's psychopathology may have played out in the unnecessary deaths of thousands of Americans in the coronavirus pandemic (at least at the time of this writing).

I'm not claiming to have read the President's mind. I'm sharing my theory of his mind with you. I can only ask you to think about what I'm saying and see if it makes sense to you.

In my opinion (which many people share), Donald Trump has Narcissistic Personality Disorder (NPD). I think it's important to make two things clear when I state this. The first is that the public tends to misunderstand and misuse psychological terms.

Here's an example: Schizophrenia does not mean a person has multiple personalities, like the movie character Sybil. Instead, schizophrenia is a disorder in which there can be hallucinations, delusions, and other breaks with reality. A person with schizophrenia can also have "negative symptoms" such as withdrawal from others and a flat mood. But the public don't use the term "schizophrenia" in this way, but instead they confuse it with multiple personality disorder.

Another example of the public not understanding psychological terms is when people say "I'm OCD" because they like to keep things neat and clean. Do you know what that really means? It means they like to keep things neat and clean. Obsessive-Compulsive Disorder, or OCD, is actually a clinical syndrome in which the person can't stop obsessing on something even though they know they should stop. Or they can't resist a compulsion, like washing their hands until they're raw and bleeding because they're afraid of germs. OCD is a much more serious condition than how people use it in everyday parlance. At its worst it can destroy lives.

There's a similar misunderstanding with Narcissistic Personality Disorder. NPD is a serious condition, just like OCD. NPD is a lot more pathological than just being a self-centered person or having a big ego. It's a personality disorder. That means that the personality is so disordered that these people perceive and experience the world in fundamentally different ways than normal people. Their world – themselves, their relationships, everything – is different than that of most people. In NPD, individuals are seen as means to an end, not as ends in themselves. People are seen as sources of supply, in other words, in terms of "what can they do for me?" People aren't perceived with their own understandable needs and motivations. If another person gives the NPD person what they want – praise, logistical help, money, etc. – they're considered a "good person." If someone denies the NPD person something they want – fails to be their source of supply – they're considered a "bad" person. It's actually pretty simple.

Here's a quote in *Psychology Today*[22] that captured the essence of the problem, and its negative implications: "If you can't conceive of other people as fully formed human beings with inner lives as vivid as (or even richer than) your own, it becomes far easier to use them as means to your own ends — that is, to exploit them."

The other point I need to make is that I have to be careful when I discuss Trump's mental condition, because I'm a psychologist. I'm only speculating about Trump's condition. I'm not saying I've conducted, as a psychologist, a clinical interview with Donald Trump the way I'd evaluate a patient, and as a result of that I have come to a professional, clinical diagnosis. There's something called the "Goldwater Rule" which was put in place decades ago when Barry Goldwater ran for president. Many mental health professionals proclaimed Goldwater to be mentally ill. Organizations like the American Psychiatric Association decided it was inappropriate for mental health professionals to make such a finding without an in-person professional clinical examination. So I'm not doing that, okay?

Finally, but very importantly, I want to say that I am speaking out in this book about the President's unhealthy mental state because I believe it presents a danger to American citizens. Indeed, I believe it also a danger to people all over the world. Mental health professionals have a "duty to warn" the public if they feel a person has psychological difficulties which present a significant risk of harm to others. I believe this is true for Donald Trump, and that is a major reason I am writing about this.

There is a book entitled The Dangerous Case of Donald Trump[23], in which 37 psychiatrists, psychologists, and other mental health experts discuss their deep concerns about Donald Trump's mental state. Its

22 - Sullivan, Glenn, PhD, "Sorry, But Your Ex Probably Isn't a Narcissist," Psychology Today, December 30, 2019. https://www.psychologytoday.com/gb/blog/acquainted-the-night/201912/sorry-your-ex-probably-isnt-narcissist

23 - https://www.amazon.ca/Dangerous-Case-Donald-Trump-Psychiatrists-dp-1250212863/dp/1250212863/ref=dp_ob_title_bk

foreword was written by the renowned psychiatrist Robert Jay Lifton. Lifton had this to say in an interview with Bill Moyers:

"We have a duty to warn on an individual basis if we are treating someone who may be dangerous to herself or to others — a duty to warn people who are in danger from that person. We feel it's our duty to warn the country about the danger of this president. If we think we have learned something about Donald Trump and his psychology that is dangerous to the country, yes, we have an obligation to say so."[24]

It's in this vein that I'm writing about my take on Donald Trump's mental health. I also want to say that I don't think my views are original, and that many mental health professionals share them. Nevertheless, they're a big reason why I moved to Canada, and as such they belong in this book.

For me, I find it quite simple to understand Mr. Trump. I actually find him boring and repetitive. I also thought his show *The Apprentice* was boring, stupid, and repetitive. Like others have said, he's just playing a similar role as president as he did on reality TV. But just because his psychology, in my view, is simple, boring, and repetitive, doesn't mean it's not extremely dangerous.

I believe the President is a very insecure man and he feels very small and weak inside. He just can't admit these feelings to himself. If he felt them, he'd be in tremendous pain. In fact, his whole personality structure is an attempt to avoid and push away these insecure feelings.

Do you know how I can tell? Because people who are secure within themselves, who feel good about who they are, don't need to constantly talk about how great they are. They don't need to say they are the best at so many things, or constantly boast of their greatness. One doesn't really need a PhD to see this.

A truly confident person will just say "thank you" when complimented and quietly enjoy their strengths. But an insecure person can react in one of two opposite ways. First, they can unfairly denigrate

---

24 - https://billmoyers.com/story/dangerous-case-donald-trump-robert-jay-lifton-bill-moyers-duty-warn/

themselves. Examples are they can minimize their accomplishments or demonstrate trouble accepting compliments from others. Similarly, they may feel never good enough and become perfectionistic as a result. Perfectionists tend to be people who feel they are in danger of being exposed as failures. Any flaw is taken as proof of their being a failure or loser. And so the only way to protect oneself from this is to be perfect. Perfectionists can achieve a lot, and therefore many people admire perfectionism. I, on the other hand, just see perfectionism as a manifestation of fear and weakness.

But the second way insecure people can manage their feelings is to head in the opposite direction and go around boasting and exaggerating their abilities. A person boasting is trying to continually compensate for their insecurity by pumping up their self-esteem. It's like having to continually inflate a damaged tire that is constantly leaking air. Now we're getting in Trump territory. Every time he boasts, his admirers see strength. Every time he boasts I, by contrast, see his weakness.

A person who can take stock of themselves and identify their strengths and weaknesses, who can admit their mistakes, and who can apologize – now that's a strong person. A person who has a damaged psyche cannot.

Question: When's the last time you heard Donald Trump apologize? He can't. He can't because he feels so bad about himself inside. He can't apologize because he doesn't have a reservoir of good self-esteem to draw upon to admit he was wrong. He cannot admit he has weaknesses. The flat tire that is his psyche is always limping along, gasping for air. Donald Trump is always trying to inflate his psyche by pumping it up with his grandiosity.

Another way to say this is that Donald Trump is a blowfish. Blowfish inflate themselves to make themselves look big to defend themselves from bigger predators. They try to make themselves look bigger because they feel threatened. They are terrified, false giants. Donald Trump is a terrified, false giant.

Actually, I think many of his followers are drawn to Trump for the same reasons – to inflate their own self-regard. Many Trump supporters, in my view, are trying to pump up their self-esteem by identifying with him. They misinterpret his boasting and putdowns of others as strength instead of weakness. And since they feel he's strong, they identify with him. They feel as though he was a part of them, and this makes them feel stronger. Think about it; many of his core supporters are people who are feeling they're losing power in current American society. They're often white, rural, uneducated males in a changing America. This political trend has been spoken about ad nauseam in the newspapers. But I don't think enough focus has been put on the psychological aspect of all this. A lot of the Trump phenomenon is just air for underinflated, leaking psyches.

The problem is that air is actually poisonous gas for the country.

Here's another scary point to consider. Because Donald Trump cannot admit to himself he doesn't know something (that would make him feel weak), he tells himself that he knows everything. He tells himself that he's an expert on everything. How many times have you heard a variation of this? Off the top of my head, I remember him saying, "I alone can fix it," (the country)[25]; or that he knows "more than the generals about ISIS."[26] I can never forget he wrote I'm "like, really smart."[27] Trump has great difficulty respecting and accepting the expertise of others, because it would mean he lacks something, and that would make him feel weak. As a result, the country will get ill-informed, often misguided policies. All of this scares me and makes me want to flee his rule.

An illustration of this at work is that Trump has consistently contradicted the healthcare experts of his own Administration about the coronavirus. I'll discuss this more in my last chapter.

***

25 - https://www.theatlantic.com/politics/archive/2016/07/trump-rnc-speech-alone-fix-it/492557/

26 - https://www.defenseone.com/policy/2016/09/trump-vs-generals/131938/

27 - https://apnews.com/2bb960fda0264c488d454632628cb193/
Trump-says-he's-'like,-really-smart,'-'a-very-stable-genius

Here's another pattern where we can see Trump's emotional difficulties in action. Because, deep down, Mr. Trump feels small and weak, he uses the psychological defense mechanism of projection to cope with his feelings. Projection is a defense mechanism whereby we take painful feelings we cannot handle and we blame, or "project" them, onto other people. We tell ourselves that we're not bad; it's they who are the bad ones. I'm not small; you're small. It's like that. This way, we get rid of these bad feelings because we're not able to feel and process them within ourselves. Projection, like grandiosity, originates from insecurity. Projection stems from the inability to cope in a healthy way with one's emotional pain. Donald Trump is a master of projection.

Here are some examples. I don't see what the height of a candidate has to do with what kind of president they would be. But their height has everything to do with things if one is preoccupied with not being small, as Trump fears he is deep down. Michael Bloomberg becomes "mini Mike," Marco Rubio is "little Marco."

Probably the most egregious (I think disgusting) example of this can be seen with the way our President perceived John McCain. Almost everyone considers that man a patriot and a war hero who sacrificed for his country in Vietnam. John McCain was shot down as a pilot in the Vietnam war. He was held as a prisoner of war for years and tortured. The North Vietnamese offered to release him early when they found out he was an admiral's son and it could earn them good publicity if they let him go. But, in what Mr. McCain felt was for the good of the country, he refused and chose to endure years of more torture.

Mr. Trump's take on Mr. McCain? Time magazine reported that Trump said: "He's not a war hero," and he said, "He wasn't a war hero because he was captured. I like people who weren't captured." [28]

To be captured, you see, is to be weak (in Trump's mind). To Trump, the idea that McCain chose to engage in combat for his country isn't significant. Trump, by contrast, of course avoided the draft by

---

28 - https://time.com/4993304/john-mccain-donald-trump-feud-remarks/

suspiciously saying he has foot problems (when asked about it, he replied, "You think I'm stupid: I wasn't going to Vietnam)."[29] But self-sacrifice doesn't matter; all that matters is being strong, and being captured is seen as weak. Strong and weak are the only moralities that apply to a narcissist like Trump.

Most people tend to see John McCain as a war hero. But this is because most people can see people for who they are, not only in terms of how they affect them. But people with NPD can only react to people along one dimension – whether they make them feel small or weak. This fundamental disparity in perception is an example of how a narcissistic person is really quite different than a regular person. They are disturbed people.

I am moving to Canada because I do not believe the President has the psychological capability to separate what is good for the country from what is good for his self-esteem. The American people chose this guy. If it happened once, it can happen again. And so the question remains, what awaits us, even if we get past Trump? Personally, I don't want to find out. I would rather not be a part of this whole mess.

Two Personal Reasons.

Someone told me that a comedian made a skit about all the Americans who said they were going to move to Canada because of the election. He talked about how Canadians' feelings were hurt because so many people said they would go to Canada after Trump was elected, but … no one came. Where were all those people? How come they decided not to come? What's wrong with Canada? he joked.

I totally relate. I felt like I was walking with a big group, and then I paused and looked around, only to discover I was all by myself. Where did everybody go?

And all of this made me start to wonder, why me? How come I actually followed through on it when so few others did? What's up with me?

---

29 - https://www.militarytimes.com/news/pentagon-congress/2019/02/27/
trumps-lawyer-no-basis-for-presidents-medical-deferment-from-vietnam/

I am reminded about what my patient said to me: I will either turn out to be a genius or an idiot.

So again, why me? It's a question I've thought long and hard about. I've come up with a few main reasons that could explain why I did it while most others didn't, although I'm sure there are more of them. Here's what I came up with.

As I explained in the previous chapter, I believe Donald Trump is a threat to both the short-term and long-term well-being of Americans and of the United States. But millions of other Americans thought this also, and it didn't compel them to move out of the country. So there must be other reasons as well.

There are four more I can identify. The first two are simple, and I'll talk about them now. The other two go deeper, and are even more personal, and I'll get to them later in the book.

1 - New York, New York.

I was born in Manhattan. I lived there until I was six years old and then I moved to Riverdale, a nice neighborhood in the Bronx. My mother remarried when I was ten and we moved to a suburb in Long Island, about an hour's drive from Manhattan. And I lived there until I went away to college. And although in college I was out of the New York City metropolitan area, I was still living in New York State.

After college I wanted to go to Northwestern University in Chicago for graduate school, but I wasn't accepted and I attended Fordham University in New York for my PhD.

Therefore, I've lived my entire life in New York. By the time I was in my 40s, I was sick and tired of living in the same place. If one has to live in only one place for an entire life, I think New York City is a great choice. In many ways, the world comes to you when you live in an international city like New York.

But although the world comes to you in New York, you still don't come to the world. I was tired of being in the same space. I'd walk down the same block in Manhattan and pass the same buildings. I would remember that in the 80s I went to a party in this building, and in the 90s a dinner in that building, and in the early 2000s I went to an event in that building. Nothing felt new. I started to feel like a caged tiger, pacing back and forth.

Moreover, I just wanted to know what it was like to experience a different culture. Most people I knew had lived somewhere else at some point. But once I had my son, I knew I was in New York City to stay, and I felt trapped.

Another factor is that I began to travel more boldly in the last several years. Instead of going to Europe, I traveled to Indonesia, to Turkey, to Israel, and to China. As a result of this, I became more confident I could thrive in different environments.

When the crisis of a Trump presidency struck, I began to reopen the possibility of living somewhere else. This was a dream I'd given up on. But, as they say, a crisis can become an opportunity. So I took this opportunity.

2 - Son/University

Another reason I wanted to become Canadian was to help my son, Jordan, who is now 15 years old. On the one hand, I'm moving away from him and won't see him as often as I could see him had I stayed in New York. I feel very bad about that, and some people have disapproved of my doing this. They have that right, and I can understand their point of view. But my thinking as a father is as follows.

I graduated from Cornell University. In American dollars, the cost of tuition for Cornell University's College of Arts and Sciences (the standard liberal arts college) is more than $55,000 USD per year. In American dollars, The University of Toronto's tuition is about $40,000 USD if you're not from Canada. But if you're from a family of a Canadian citizen or permanent resident, the cost is only $4,500 USD.

Although rankings vary, the University of Toronto and Cornell are both ranked very highly and similarly (18th and 19th in the world, according to the 2019 Times Higher Education survey)[30].

Also, if Jordan attends university in Canada, he'll have the benefit of being exposed to a foreign culture, which I think is a good thing.

Furthermore, there are no private universities in Canada. If you are a Canadian, you pay these kinds of relatively low rates at any university. Of course, as with other things, Canadians complain about their burdensome university costs. At these times I clench my teeth to keep my mouth shut. Remember, as I said earlier, life is relative.

My son Jordan and I worked out a schedule together where I'll come to NYC one weekend a month and he'll come to Toronto one weekend a month. So I will at a minimum see him for quality time at least once every two weeks.

One final, but hardly insignificant, point. I took my son to be tested for his Canadian medical exam along with mine. This was to facilitate my sponsoring him to be a permanent resident of Canada. My immigration lawyer quipped that if he attends university in Canada, he'll end up becoming a Canadian citizen faster than I will. I believe I'm going to be becoming a citizen of a more stable, less acrimonious, and more kind country, while still not giving up my American citizenship. I don't know what's going to happen with the United States in the future. But unlike those who just "hope for the best," I took action to help ensure the safety and well-being of my child. And not only for my son, but perhaps for the generations of Shainbarts still unborn.

As I mentioned, I'll discuss the other reasons I moved to Canada, which are much more personal, later in this book. But, for now, I want to "get into it" and describe what it was like for me to try to become Canadian. Oh boy. You better sit down for this.

---

30 - https://www.timeshighereducation.com/world-university-rankings/2020/world-ranking#!/page/0/length/25/sort_by/rank/sort_order/asc/cols/stats

3

So You Want to Become Canadian?
My Story

This is my particular journey to becoming Canadian. It's my story, but it contains many of the requirements that the Canadian government expects people to meet before they can become Canadian. Because it's my story, some of the requirements may not apply to you, and inversely, you may have to meet certain requirements I didn't have to (there is an overview, written by a Canadian immigration attorney, describing the various programs and pathways that exist to become Canadian in Chapter 5).

I must point out that I'm not an immigration attorney and I'm not claiming to be providing comprehensive, precisely accurate immigration criteria. Moreover, the criteria the Canadian government uses to evaluate people for citizenship does change. Therefore, this book isn't a replacement for hiring your own immigration attorney or even going to the relevant Canadian websites for information. I'm just going to describe some of the criteria that they employ. I'll also point you to some websites that you may find helpful, as well as giving you my advice on whether you should hire your own immigration attorney (yes!) and how to choose a good one (very important).

My Journey

The first thing I did, immediately after the 2016 election, was go on the internet and research the possibility of becoming licensed as a psychologist in Ontario. I figured that if I couldn't continue my career, moving to Canada would be a non-starter. So what would be involved in this? I was fairly confident and hopeful, because I had a PhD in Clinical Psychology from a solid university, more than twenty years of experience in the field and I was in good standing (never having been brought up on ethics charges, sued, etc.). I'd taught and supervised various students in training to become psychologists and therapists. I knew my credentials were solid and extensive and my experience was substantial.

What I didn't know was that I was entering Alice's Wonderland. It's a realm where the fact I had extensive experience in the field as a psychologist would become a *liability* in my becoming licensed in Ontario. In its effort to ensure they only allow psychologists with sufficient experience to be allowed to practice, the organization that does the accreditation across states and provinces, Association of State and Provincial Psychologists (ASPP), uses a procedure that favors candidates with *less* experience and actually penalizes those with more experience. It's nuts.

The amount of paperwork I had to submit was overwhelming. I have little patience with rigid, unnecessary, and stupid procedures. It probably has to do with my Meyers-Briggs personality type, which is INFP, or "Mediator". I'm a concept/ideas person, not a logistics and details person. If everyone was like me, the trains would stop working. But at least we would all conceptually understand why the trains stopped working.

But I know this about myself. As a psychologist, a core belief of mine is that self-awareness can be harnessed into a tremendous advantage in life. Therefore, I knew from the beginning I'd hate this whole bureaucratic process and I'd want to rebel against it. I knew that this aspect of my personality would work against me.

So I decided to view this as a personal challenge. No matter what ridiculous and lengthy procedures they threw at me, I was not going to let it stop me. I would meet and master whatever they wanted from me. Any bureaucratic requirement was going to be an opportunity to demonstrate my willpower. That's how I looked at it.

Bureaucracy and paperwork became an opponent to be defeated, not a source of exasperation to make me give up. I think that's one reason I succeeded in this quest to get to Canada while many other people quit.

But it almost killed me.

After months and months of submitting transcripts, copies of my NY State license, a letter showing that I'm in good standing, and tons of other documentation, my application was stalled for three months and, for a while, it even looked like I was going to be rejected. The ASPP had counted the number of hours that I saw patients under supervision in my clinical internship at Nassau County Medical Center on Long Island (properly pronounced "Nasaww Countee Medicahl Centah"). To get licensed in NY State, you need a certain number of clinical hours under supervision. The paperwork for this needs to be submitted to the state to be licensed as a psychologist in New York.

I completed my internship in 1989. I had to contact NY State to get this ancient information for Ontario. I had my doubts whether a record of it still existed, but fortunately New York State had kept a photocopy of these records. Thank God. I was in luck.

Or so I thought. Somehow, the ASPP told me the paperwork didn't show I had sufficient hours. Yet I knew I'd completed them. Newer applicants had all these records stored more accurately via computer, but with older applications like mine, the record-keeping was not electronic. They were less accurate, relying on decades-old paper trails.

I spoke my mind, albeit politely, to the woman from ASPP. I said, "Do you mean that people fresh out of school, with very little experience, but who have their internship year recorded by computer, are favored over people like me with twenty years' experience in the field?"

She simply replied, "Yes."

I then said, "And this is all done to make sure that the applicants have enough experience to practice psychology?"

She said, "Yes."

I said, "That makes no sense!"

She said, and I will never forget this as long as I live: "Well, that's the way we do it."

It's not that she was mean-spirited. She just was unable or unwilling to question the procedures. In fact, she tried to help. I spoke with her some more, and she said if I could get my supervisor from 1989 to sign off that I'd completed the hours (which I had completed) then that would be an acceptable solution. I pointed out this was from almost 30 years ago. What if she was *dead*? Anyway, she googled my old supervisor while I was waiting on the phone, and found her alive and still practicing in Brooklyn.

I'd met with this supervisor an hour a week for a year. I'd also been friendly with this woman. I even went with my sister to her home for Shabbat dinner (she was also Jewish). She lived in the same neighborhood in Queens as my sister.

And so, the next day, I called the supervisor. To my disappointment and some surprise, she had difficulty remembering me. I had to keep describing myself. By contrast, later that day I spoke to my sister, who'd met her only once. My sister said, "Of course I remember her. We had dinner there." Yet the supervisor barely remembered me, even though she met with me frequently for over a year.

Great. I said I could prove I was who I said I was, etc.

This was the beginning of a recurrent theme in my journey to become Canadian: proving that I was who I said I was to people. Throughout this process, in various ways, I was placed in situations in which I had to demonstrate who I was in ways I never had to before. Some examples include proving that I was capable of speaking English; proving I was an experienced, fully credentialed psychologist; proving that I was indeed a white man, and so on. Mark this theme; I'll return to it throughout the book.

Anyway, the supervisor finally agreed to sign the paper for ASPP. I waited two weeks. Nothing. I emailed her, twice. No response. I was getting worried. Finally she emailed me back. She said she was "not comfortable" signing the paper.

My God. My whole application, my whole plan to move to Canada, was going to be stopped because I'd failed to make a lasting impression on a supervisor I knew in 1989.

I was miserable.

I thought about what to do. I called another supervisor from the internship, who was not my full supervisor, unlike this woman. He was the only person still working there that I worked with. We spoke on the phone. I remembered him as a young, cool, warm and genuine guy.

He told me he was about to retire. Dear God, how time passes. I felt old.

And yet, despite being old, here I was, scrambling to prove I had sufficient experience in the field!

I also called a guy who was also starting his career in psychology in 1989 who worked closely with the memory-challenged female supervisor. He'd been close with her, and I was sure he could vouch for me and remind her who I was.

Unlike her, he remembered me well, and we schmoozed for a bit. Then I told him about my situation and how ridiculous it was and asked for his help. I told him some of the specifics of my clinical hours and the whole difficulty.

He didn't think it was ridiculous at all. This guy could keep the trains running on time. Definitely not an INFP type. He went on in great detail about how the ASPP system made perfect sense and how it was important to closely regulate people coming into the field of psychology. Inside, I became angry, but didn't say anything. He discussed the specific numbers about my hours, in a way that I hadn't even thought about. In a way that I probably couldn't think about even if I wanted to. His attention to detail was both impressive and annoying as hell. He couldn't see the forest for the trees, but he could accurately count all the individual trees in the forest. As we neared the end of the phone call, he expressed reluctance to speak with the supervisor on my behalf. I don't know why.

Frankly, I was disgusted.

But ...

But ...

Then I thought about all the specific details he described about my clinical hours. I never would've thought about it in that level of detail if it wasn't for him.

In reviewing all these details, it dawned on me that I'd already documented sufficient hours to meet their criteria. I realized the ASPP had miscalculated it. I checked over the numbers again, and they held up. I called ASPP and presented them with all these facts. The ASPP woman said I was correct, that it had been their mistake, and I did have sufficient hours. Therefore I could go on and eventually have my credentials approved to work as a psychologist in Ontario.

This entire stupid and scary process had delayed me by two to three months.

But I persevered. Baruch Hashem. That means Thank God in Hebrew. The project was still a go.

***

Next, I found and called a Canadian immigration lawyer in Toronto. I told her I was looking into the possibility of becoming a Canadian citizen because of Trump. I don't remember the particulars – it was three years ago – but I know we discussed my case in enough detail that I felt I had a shot at pulling it off. So I decided to take a trip to Toronto – my first trip to Toronto in my life – and meet with her to discuss things in more depth, in-person.

I also wanted to visit Toronto to see if I liked it. I knew nothing about the place. I'd never met anyone in my entire life from there, with one exception. He was a client I'd stopped working with many years ago. He'd grown up in Toronto and later moved to NYC. I remember he described it as a very clean city, kind of boring, very organized, with modern, rectangular skyscrapers. I remember I drew a mental image of that in my mind, but I don't think I thought about Toronto ever again after that.

I wanted my then eleven-year-old son Jordan to come with me on this first trip to Toronto so that he'd be fully involved in this decision. If I ended up doing this, I'd be living away from him, and in another country to boot. I had very mixed feelings about leaving him, which I'll explain in a moment. But, regardless of what I felt, *how he felt* was very important. If he was against my dream of going to Canada, I wouldn't pursue it. My dream would die then and there. I'd be sad about that, and a little angry (not at him, but because of my disappointment), but he comes first. I wouldn't ever act in a way that would cause my child to feel I abandoned him, even if I didn't see it that way. I knew that how he viewed it, not how I viewed it, would determine how he'd respond to it psychologically. And that would determine how I'd respond. I wouldn't hurt my son. This was my priority.

I told him I wanted to see Toronto with him and, if he felt it was too distant, I wouldn't move there. Although it's only a one-hour flight from New York City, I wanted him to experience the trip for himself and see if it would feel too far away. And so we flew, and he was surprised and excited the plane ride felt so short. He'd flown several times before, but those were longer flights. For example, I'd taken him to Scotland, to the Grand Canyon, and to Vancouver. In 2013 I took him to Vancouver because it was my favorite city in the world and I wanted him to see it. I wanted to show him there were some very cool and beautiful places in the world besides New York to live in. I had no idea at that time I'd ever consider moving to Canada (I mean, Obama was the president).

As he was prone to do, Jordan got sick in Vancouver with a stomach bug and ended up in the emergency room. He was miserable, but we both enjoyed how kind and caring and *nice* the Canadian doctors were.

But what I remembered most about that trip to Vancouver was that everyone else was waiting to be seen with their government health cards. The administrative staff, however, told me that because I was paying for the visit, unlike the Canadians who were using their government health insurance, I'd be seen first – before everyone else. I said

"How very American!" to them when they told me about this. I thought what they did was wrong, because as a liberal, blue-state Democrat, I don't think healthcare should be prioritized to those who have or spend more money. I let them take me and my son first, however. I mean, I'm not an idiot.

At any rate, on this trip to Toronto, we stayed in Bond Place Hotel, in Yonge-Dundas Square. Yonge-Dundas Square has been described as "Toronto's answer to Times Square." If it is, it's one sucky answer. It's actually more like Toronto's answer to a small sliver of Times Square. Sometimes, during a slow afternoon, you can walk through it and not even realize you've entered it. That's not possible in Times Square – any time you go through it, you know you are in a different and very intense place.

The hotel room was awful: small and expensive (that part did indeed remind me of NYC). It had no dresser to store your clothes in the room. Jordan (and I) thought we were being ripped off.

But the hotel was in the heart of things, and we walked around. What was it like? Well, first of all, it was *fucking freezing*. I had never been colder in my whole life. I felt like my bones could freeze and snap off. Nevertheless, we were excited to go exploring and we bundled up. It was painful to walk outside, but Jordan was a trooper. We passed the old City Hall and the iconic "Toronto" sign by the ice-skating rink in Nathan Phillips Square. We also went to a cool place called "Snakes and Lattes" and played board games. It was fun.

I brought Jordan with me to meet my Canadian immigration lawyer. The office was classically and expensively decorated, radiating old wealth that would be at home in the Harvard Club. I wanted him involved as much as possible, if just to observe, even if he didn't understand all of it. I found the meeting with the lawyer and her assistant somewhat confusing. I found the whole meeting also vague and underwhelming. But overall it seemed like there was a path forward. I found out I had to get one year of Canadian work experience to acquire enough points to qualify for Canadian permanent residency under a program called "Express Entry." My being a psychologist with a PhD was a category favored for consideration for immigration under NAFTA. Moreover, the more education one had, the more points one accumulated for acceptance in Canada. I was happy about that. I often felt getting a PhD did not pay off financially in my career, considering how many more years and sacrifice it required compared with a Master's of Social Work degree or other therapist degrees with far less education. At least this time I was finally getting some mileage out of my PhD.

I should point out it was pretty easy for me to decide, if I was going to move to Canada, Toronto would be the place for me. As I mentioned, I needed to get a year of Canadian work experience. And I also needed to be near my son, who'd remain in New York. There are two large Canadian cities near New York: Toronto and Montreal. I don't speak French, therefore it seemed clear I should concentrate my job search in Toronto.

Fortunately, I liked Toronto. It was fucking freezing (did I mention that?) but it was fun to be in a new city, a big city. It was much cleaner and gentler and slower than NYC, but it still felt like a decent-sized city, with a lot of stuff to do. I didn't think it was the greatest place ever: it wasn't beautiful like Vancouver or historic like Rome, and it didn't have the gorgeous and interesting architecture of Chicago. But it was still fun and pleasant, and I felt I could be happy there, as long as I wasn't too cold.

Jordan also approved. I felt really relieved. This project was a go.

4
My Musings on Canada and Toronto

As I write this now (2020), I've spent between two and three years living in Toronto, although I've been going back and forth to New York until quite recently. I wanted to share my impressions and experiences of Toronto. Of course, this is completely subjective; one man's heaven is another man's hell, and vice versa.

I really like Toronto. There are reasons it ranks so highly among the world's most livable cities. Toronto ranked #16 in the world according to The 2019 Mercer Quality of Living Survey.[31] The survey is done every year, and it ranked more than 200 cities. Ten categories involving quality of life were evaluated. Some of these included: political and social, economic, consumer goods, education, public services and transportation, socio-cultural, and housing.

Toronto also kicks butt in the quality of life rankings compared with any American city. In fact, it's ranked #2 in all of North America, according to Mercer:

Top ten cities in North America for quality of living
1. Vancouver, Canada
2. Toronto, Canada
3. Ottawa, Canada

---

31 - https://mobilityexchange.mercer.com/Insights/quality-of-living-rankings

4. Montreal, Canada

5. Calgary, Canada

6. San Francisco, USA

7. Boston, USA

8. Honolulu, USA

9. New York, USA

10. Seattle, USA

Actually, while we're at it, let me report on a few things about how Canada ranks compared with the United States. *US News* and *World Report* stated the worldwide rankings of countries in terms of quality of life. Quality of life was measured according to nine factors: political stability, safety, public education, public health, affordability, job market, economic stability, family friendliness, and income equality.

Canada ranked #1 in the world for the fifth year in a row. They reported that Canada ranked in the top ten of all countries in all of the categories except affordability, where Asian countries do best. The United States' ranking for quality of life? #15.[32]

Anyway, back to Toronto, which the actor Peter Ustinov called "New York run by the Swiss." This quote is consistent with my experience. Toronto is kind of like New York, but it's run more efficiently, with less stress and fewer annoyances.

In my opinion, Toronto's restaurant scene is on par with New York, which is quite an accomplishment. Toronto is often regarded as the most ethnically diverse city in the world (New York is no slouch either, especially its borough of Queens, which is often called the most diverse place on earth). In Toronto there are so many types of cuisines, especially Asian foods. There's less of everything there, because it's roughly one-third the size of New York. But, at least for me, I don't need so much of everything, as long as it's there.

Toronto does have far fewer art museums than New York and a much smaller theater scene. It lacks the dense population of New York, and therefore lacks the energy of New York. This is both a blessing and

---

32 - https://www.usnews.com/news/best-countries/quality-of-life-rankings

a curse. If you want to be in a place that's a leader in the worldwide art scene, for example, New York is the place, not Toronto. However, while it may not be as exciting as New York, Toronto is a lot more pleasant. You don't feel like you've been through a war in getting around Toronto (relative to NYC). You don't have to look at mountains of garbage bags everywhere. You don't have to constantly see rats in the streets and subways. There are relatively few cockroaches (again, at least compared with NYC). The subways do not reek of urine. And so on.

New York has become cleaner since the hellish days of the 1970s and 1980s. But Toronto is still significantly cleaner. It's just so nice to walk around and not have your senses assaulted with filth and noise.

On the other hand, Toronto lacks, for the most part, a strong character, in my view. There are some wonderful and interesting neighborhoods. I love Kensington Market, for example. Kensington Market is a neighborhood full of shops selling all kinds of ethnic foods, with offbeat stores. It has smaller, older buildings, and has a history, like many parts of New York, of being populated by different ethnic groups at different times. And in the warmer months, Kensington Market's streets are full of street performers. So fun!

But much of Toronto is nondescript, and I find much of the architecture banal. Many older buildings have been torn down and a bland modernness pervades instead.

To sum it up, Toronto is a very good place to live. There's enough interesting and fun stuff to do here. Sometimes I wish it was a bit more dynamic and quirky. However, my biggest feeling by far, coming from New York City, is one of relief. I enjoy living in Toronto: the people are generally civilized and kind, the city clean, and there's plenty to do. I don't feel bored and I don't feel overstimulated either. It's "just right" in Toronto.

The truth is, when I get off the plane in Toronto, I feel happy and more relaxed than when I get off the plane in New York. I like it here. You know the saying "It's a nice place to visit but I wouldn't want to live there?" Well, for me, Toronto is the opposite. It's a nice place to live, and New York is the nice place to visit. I like the way my life is now.

***

I'm at the airport in Toronto, heading back to New York. I'm very late for my flight. There is a long security line ahead of me. I realize I am going to probably miss my flight. I have a pit forming in my stomach. I'm uncomfortable, but I bring myself to ask the people in front of me if I can go ahead of them. I'm worried they will get annoyed at me, and perhaps refuse. I'm used to this possibility, because I'm from New York.

I ask, and the couple in front of me smile and say "Sure!" I'm relieved. But there's still a long line ahead of me. Then the people in front of this couple overhear me, and they say to me, "You can go ahead of us too," and they wave me ahead of them. I'm surprised and grateful. This keeps happening; people in front keep reaching out to me, one after the other, each suggesting I go ahead of them. Some just nod and wave me ahead, having seen me coming. It's awesome. One guy starts talking to me a bit, and I tell him I'm from New York and trying to become Canadian. He says, "What's the matter – you're angry about Trump?" I say, "My friends are angry about Trump. I'm just terrified and escaping."

Finally, I'm about five people from the front. The person behind me urges me to ask the remaining few people ahead of me if I can go ahead of them. But I just can't do it anymore at this point. I feel like I'm asking for too much. I'm almost there anyway.

I'm still stressed because I might miss my flight, although my odds have improved greatly. I get to the scanning machine and the officer tells me I have to get rid of the bottle of water in my backpack, which I'd forgotten all about. I look to throw it out but don't see any garbage bin. So I pull it out and start gulping down the water as fast as I can. I then put my stuff on the belt and it goes through the machine. After it comes through the machine, I quickly start picking my stuff up and rush to put on my backpack.

As I'm doing so, the person behind me on the line (who was the guy I spoke to earlier) says to me: "If you can drink beer like you can gulp that water, you can be one of us." I was delighted.

Then I ran like hell to my plane. I just made it.

In routine circumstances, like this one, this demonstration of group kindness doesn't happen in New York City, at least in my experience. Great kindness in NYC was quite apparent in the days after 9/11, and it can come out during other emergency situations. New Yorkers tend to be there for each when they need to be. But under routine conditions, it's often every person for themselves. NYC is one crowded, tough place. I guess it has to be, given the density, or it wouldn't function.

This experience at the Toronto airport warms my heart. People treating each other as I think people should be treated, with kindness and generosity, on a routine basis. I tell myself I think I'm going to like living here.

A Tale of Two Cities

The subway is the best way to see the cultural difference between New York and Toronto. The two environments are similar, as they are both subway cars and stations. The Toronto cars are nicer and cleaner, the seats upholstered. The stations are litter-free. Recycling bins are everywhere. New York run by the Swiss. But physically, overall, they are similar enough.

The difference which really stands out, because the two environments look the same, is in how the people act.

You can strike up a conversation on the subway with a stranger in New York, no problem. If you do that on the TTC (the Toronto transit system), most people will think you're weird. That's one illustration of this cultural difference.

New Yorkers are loud on the train, speaking in loud voices, laughing loudly, and basically often disregard their fellow passengers. Almost every subway ride is interrupted by people asking for money. Some of them with musical instruments. Most of all I dread "Showtime," when young men play hip hop music and start dancing and swinging on the poles in the train car. Many times their body parts have come whizzing by my face and body. I hate riding the subway in New York.

By contrast, I love riding the Toronto subway. I can relax on it. People are quiet and respectful. The very few that talk keep the volume of their voices low. There's far less panhandling, and when it occurs, it typically feels less threatening, (even more polite!). There is no "Showtime." The Toronto subway is … soothing.

I am sensitive to noise, so the difference between Toronto and NYC may not be as great for everyone. But, for me, it's a small miracle to be able to relax and focus on the train. Torontonians can complain all they want about their subway. As a former New Yorker, I love the TTC.

***

I'm at Cineplex Cinemas at Yonge-Dundas Square in Toronto. It's at one of those fancy theaters where they have waiters come to take your food order and serve you during the movie. I don't care about the fancy food thing; I only picked it because I wanted to see the film at that specific time. Anyway, I'm already inside the cineplex, but the previews have begun and I'm trying to find my particular theater. The usher/waiter comes over to help me and starts walking with me. He says, in this overly pleasant and overly polite sing-song voice, "I'm saw-ree (this is the Canadian pronunciation of "sorry") but the movie is almost starting, so I need to take your food order as soon as possible. We're only allowed to be in the theater for the first thirty minutes of the movie. I'm saw-ree."

I just keep looking at him for a couple of seconds, as we continue to walk. I then say, "Only for the first thirty minutes?" He replies, "Yes, that's correct." Then I say, "Well, can you at least sit next to me for the first thirty minutes? I know you have to go after thirty minutes, but can you at least watch the first half-hour with me?"

I'm enjoying this. I know most New Yorkers would instinctively realize I was just joking. But I wait to see what he'll do with it. Without missing a beat he says: "I'm saw-ree, I can't. I need to take your order as soon as possible because we're not allowed to be in the theater after the first thirty minutes."

I respond: "I understand. But can you at least sit and watch the film with me for half an hour? I know you have to leave after that."

"I'm saw-ree, but I'm not allowed to be in the theater after thirty minutes, so if you could please … ."

I can't stand this anymore. I interrupt him and say: "I'm joking!"

Immediately, in the exact same overly polite overly pleasant voice, he says: "Oh, I know you're joking. But I'm saw-ree, I'm only allowed to be in the theater for the first thirty minutes so if you could please try to place your order as soon as possible … ."

This was an early lesson in Canadian culture. Most Canadians have a better sense of humor than this guy, but this story does serve as a caricature of something I've sensed. What is it? A greater formality, and greater sense of reserve, certainly compared with New Yorkers. And, from my perspective, an excessive dedication to apologizing and to following procedures. It may be stereotypical, but I really do believe there's something to this stereotype.

A Torontonian client told me this joke:

How do you get a Canadian to apologize?

Step on his foot.

On Language

I was born in Manhattan and I lived my entire life in New York State. All 56 years of it. I speak only one language: English. So naturally, the Canadian government required that I take a three-hour test of my ability to speak English.

The test was given in Manhattan, and everyone put on their head-phones and sat in a cubicle. The testing was done by computer. Four areas were assessed: speaking, listening, reading, and writing.

I took the elevator up to the floor in the Manhattan office building where the English exam was being given. There was one other person in the elevator with me. He looked at me and said, "I have a PhD and I only speak one language, English." I replied, "I have a PhD, and I only speak one language, English." It was funny and felt good to have some validation of the ridiculousness of the moment.

In the interest of full disclosure, I can in fact throw a few Spanish words together. But I most certainly can't speak Spanish. In high school, I struggled mightily with Spanish and it was my worst subject. Moreover, I hated my 10th-grade Spanish teacher, Ms. Principi. Which made me hate Spanish more. That was one vicious cycle of hatred from hell: Ms. Prinicipi and the Spanish language. Often, when I was bored and confused in Spanish class, Ms. Principi would pause her teaching to torture me and say "Esteban, estas en amardo? (Stephen, are you in love?)" And then she'd repeat it, "Esteban, estas en amardo?"

One time, during an exam, out of nowhere she singled me out and loudly accused me of cheating (I wasn't). Boy, I hated Spanish. Maybe I have more in common with Trump after all. But I hate Spanish just because I struggle with foreign languages (and I hated Ms. Principi). If you're not Ms. Principi, it's nothing personal. If you are Ms. Principi, it is. But it's not that I'm suspicious of Spanish-speaking people. That's the difference between me and Trump.

Anyway, around this time in high school, my parents liked to go to this Spanish restaurant for dinner. I was really something then. I'd instituted a long-standing contingency plan to deal with this potentially awful situation. I told my parents that if they were going to the Spanish restaurant to please tell me first and I'd stay home and make myself a tuna sandwich (toasted on white bread with mayonnaise and lettuce). This plan always worked brilliantly, and I was always content with the results.

However, one day it was my stepbrother Richard's birthday. My mother, my stepfather Marty, my sister, Richard, and I piled in the car. We were going to dinner to celebrate. We drove for about ten minutes, and then I thought to ask, "Where are we going?" My mother said, "To the Spanish restaurant."

"Take me home! You know the policy," I exclaimed. In one of the few times I remember my mother saying something that I look back on as sensible, she said, "Stephen, you're being ridiculous. We're going to the Spanish restaurant to celebrate Richard's birthday, and you're coming along and that's that."

"Fine!" I said. The waiter came to take our order, and when it was my turn, he asked me what I'd have. I replied "I will have absolutely nothing."

Then, after a few minutes, I went to the payphone booth in the back (this was circa 1980) and called my best friend Alan Saperstein to spend the next half-hour complaining about my captivity by the Spaniards.

It may be hard to believe, but I do have a point here. The point is: I'm pathetic in my ability to speak anything except English. But there I was, being tested on my only method of communication for three hours.

Even if you were born and raised in fucking England, Canada will make you go through the same test of your ability to speak English. Moreover, the exam is incredibly boring. In the listening section, one of the stories had to do with a person who signs up for a membership card at a Costco-type store and is entitled to certain membership benefits. They were described and we were asked about the specific benefits of these cardholders. This was after hours of my being tested on my ability to speak English. I thought I was going to lose my mind from boredom. I'm not a details person at all (I can't recall if I mentioned that) and I tried my hardest to focus, but it was like swimming upstream. Membership benefits ... I mean, who really cares?

Adding insult to injury, I also noted with irony the 20-year-olds administering the English test to me were speaking broken English with thick foreign accents.

Anyway, the scoring is such that you get all possible credit if you get above ten on a 12-point scale. On speaking, reading, and listening, I received either an 11 or 12, so I got the maximum credit.

I scored a seven on my ability to write English, however. Seven is the slightest bit above the norm for the average immigrant taking the English test. WTF? This really bothered me, because I consider myself a decent writer. After all, I'm writing this, aren't I? Either I'm way off in my assessment of my ability to write in English, or the test is.

The test for writing English involved composing simulated work emails. My view of such emails is they are to be perfunctory at best. So I wrote concise emails. My best guess is that I was too brief on the emails to do well on their scoring system. Who knows? Anyway, my lawyer told me not to worry about it, that my total score on the overall test was fine. But I'm still bothered by that writing score. I certainly hope you think my writing is better than that testing agency does. I'll leave it up to you to decide.

I had to wait a month for the results, adding another month to the process. Well, at least I passed, right?

I Am Not an Asian Man Who Was Surgically Altered to Look Like a White Man

I started visiting Toronto more regularly to become familiar with the city; it was exciting to be able to hop on a plane for an hour and explore my potential new home. And for companionship, I would go on dates with Torontonian women I met through dating apps.

One of my first dates was with a Chinese-Canadian woman in her mid-forties. She grew up in China but lived in Canada for about 20 years. We'd been texting for a few days, and then I flew up to Toronto. She said she'd show me some of the city. She picked me up in her car and drove to a place called The Beaches, although Torontonians also call it The Beach. Whatever. Kind of like how they use kilometers for distance, Celsius for temperature, but pounds for weight, and inches for height, and square feet for apartment sizes.

Sometimes Canadians give me shit for how Americans, unlike the rest of the world, still don't use the metric system. Fair enough, but at least we don't have this mish-mash of indecision over what to use. At least we have the balls to use our own coherent system. The measurement systems of the USA and Canada are representative of each nation's character, I believe. Canadians, in my opinion, have a tendency toward accommodation, and Americans toward stubborn independence. So the USA uses a system at odds with the entire world, and Canada lacks a coherent system because it's so busy accommodating the USA and the rest of the world. The character of both nations brings their people costs and benefits. We'll see this later in my chapter on how each country dealt with, or failed to deal with, the coronavirus pandemic.

Anyway, at least the Beaches or the Beach was a beach, albeit on a lake, not like the ocean in NYC. Then we went to a place called EverGreen Brickworks for coffee. We had a nice time talking, and it was a pleasant and comfortable day. For a first date, especially a long first date, it was pretty good, I thought.

I flew back home to NYC. The next day I called her up and asked her if I could see her again. "I don't know," she responded.

I was surprised. "What's up? Why?" I asked.

"There's something strange about you," she replied.

Puzzled, I said "What?"

And she said, "Well, how do I know you are who you say you are? I mean, you are saying you are this guy from New York who wants to move to Toronto, but what if you're not? What if you're lying? How do I know you're not some imposter?"

Unlike her, I was innocent and trusting, and I said, "Well, I can take a picture of my passport and show it to you."

She said okay. I did so. "Feel better?" I asked.

She said she did somewhat, but she asked if I had any more proof I was who I said I was. I should've stopped right there, if not before. But I said I had my birth certificate, and it shows I was born in Manhattan. I sent her a photo of my birth certificate. I was being a schmuck. I don't think she was collecting my documents for identity fraud, but another person easily could've been. Did I mention I was acting like schmuck?

I asked her if she was reassured. She said: "Okay, but there are other strange things about you."

"Like what?"

She said, "Well, for one thing, you don't look like a regular white guy."

"What do you mean?"

"Well, you look kind of Asian."

Oy. I was flabbergasted. No one in my entire life has ever thought that I was Asian and not white. I was getting both annoyed (finally!) and beginning to grasp the absurdity of the situation. I tried to exaggerate the ridiculousness of her suspicions so she would see they were silly and relax. Toward that end I said: "So what do you think: that I'm secretly an Asian guy, and I was surgically altered to look like a white guy just so I could fool you on our date?"

There was a pause. Finally she said: "It's possible."

Then I said this wasn't going to work out and wished her luck.

***

As I said earlier, my lawyer informed me I had to acquire one year of Canadian work experience before I could apply for permanent residency, to obtain enough points to be admitted into Canada under their "Express Entry" program. Calling it "Express Entry" was a cruel irony. Glacially paced entry would be a better name for the program, in my case anyway.

I had to find a job in Toronto. I didn't know a single person in the city, however. I just went around asking EVERYONE I talked to if they knew ANYONE in Toronto. I also looked up on Psychology Today some Toronto psychologists and called a few asking if they knew about any job opportunities. I'm a bit introverted and dislike networking. Yet, for this endeavor, I did something I hadn't done before; I just put my uncomfortable feelings about networking aside and plunged forward.

Even in building my practice, I'd procrastinate when I needed to network. But I was relentlessly determined in my goal to become

Canadian, and I simply refused to give much attention to my discomfort. Looking back at this now, it shows me how very determined I was.

I'd given a talk at a psychology conference sponsored by an organization in New York I was part of called FamilyKind. I was part of a panel of three people on how being a child of divorce affected our career choice. I spoke with another psychologist in New York, and he told me a psychologist named Barbara Jo Fiddler had presented at a similar type of conference the year before, and she was from Toronto. I called her and asked if she had any ideas about how I could find a psychologist job in Toronto. She was incredibly helpful and gave me the names of a few people and places. I followed up on them like a laser beam.

One of these people was a director of a group practice in Toronto. I explained my whole situation. He was very affable and invited me up to meet with him in Toronto. I went, and we liked each other. He said he'd hire me after I got approved by the bureaucracy to practice in Ontario.

After I finally survived the bureaucratic bullshit of being allowed to practice in Ontario, which was nightmarish, I began working in Toronto in November 2017. It was exactly one year after the election. Things were moving along!

Stephen and the Kinky X-Ray Man

Getting a physical exam is part of the process of applying to become a permanent resident of Canada. And that's fair enough. All I ask is that they use doctors who can recognize basic human body parts. I mean, the kind that everyone has. Is that too much to expect?

My son and I went in April 2019 to get the physical exam. There were two doctors' offices in NYC approved to do the Canada exam. I went to the location in Manhattan's Chinatown. I'm planning on sponsoring my son for citizenship eventually, and so my immigration lawyer advised me to get him a physical exam as well. So there we were, being examined. We peed in our cups, the whole thing, etc. Then I had to go to another place down the street to get a chest X-ray. After they processed those results, I had to make sure they were submitted as part of my application for my Canadian permanent residency. I was told that I could be approved within six months of my submission, assuming nothing went wrong.

Assuming nothing went wrong. Ha.

I waited for two months. And then … I remember that morning quite well. I remember staying at an Airbnb. I woke up and thought to myself "Stephen, maybe you should dare to think positively. Maybe nothing will go wrong with the application, and within six months you will be a Canadian PR (permanent resident). Why does something have to go wrong? Maybe things can work out sometimes. Think positively (and stop thinking like a neurotic Jew from New York). Deal with the possibility of good news."

You may remember from the beginning of this book that expecting things to work out smoothly isn't my natural tendency. But I was trying to evolve as a person. Boy, did I get mine for trying to do that.

Still lying in bed, I checked email on my phone. There it was: an email from Canadian immigration. It said there were several problems with my application. One problem involved inconclusive medical exam results. They didn't specify what they meant by that.

I'd ended up switching immigration attorneys some time before this. I wasn't happy with the first one and their confusing and vague feedback. My new immigration attorneys said I would have to go back to the original doctor in Chinatown and find out what the medical problem was.

The administrative people and the doctors in the medical office were pleasant. They said there was a "shadow" on my chest X-ray, and I had to go get another chest X-ray. And then I'd have to wait to get the results and resubmit them to Canadian immigration. It took around a month to get all this done. Also … "a shadow?" I thought I'm probably fine, but what if it's some kind of growth? Cancer? I actually didn't worry about it all that much; I primarily just WANTED TO GET IT DONE, and stop LOSING TIME.

Anyway, I went to get the second chest X-ray. The X-ray technician put a sticker next to my left nipple. This was, he told me, a "nipple marker." As he put it on me, I softly said to him, "You know, this is kind of kinky."

The results came in a week or so later. The "shadow" was my nipple.

I actually have another one, but they haven't found it yet.

Air Travel

Much of my income was still coming from my private practice in NYC. As a result, I had to fly back and forth between New York City and Toronto sooooo many times. At first I thought it was cool, like I was living the life of a jetsetter. But within a few months I really began to hate flying. It wasn't only the one-hour flight; that was the least of it. Getting to and from the airports was awful; it was time-consuming and a waste of time. Moreover, flights were often very delayed or, especially in the winter, cancelled. On a good day the trip was about four hours door to door, but it could be much more than that.

When you fly a few times a year, and you're not rich, you can take a taxi to the airport. When you do it all the time, and you're not rich, the cost adds up. Especially in New York City. So I usually had to go the slow, cheap way. It was terrible. Subways, buses, etc. Did I mention how I feel about the New York public transit system?

Flying often, and paying for it yourself, is incredibly expensive. Each roundtrip was about $300 USD. I looked to see if the airlines offered significant discounts for people like me who flew the same route frequently. I was unpleasantly surprised to find there were none. People would often tell me "you must have gotten so many frequent flier miles!" Umm, no. The flight is only about 400 miles, so the miles just don't add up.

I used up sooooo much of my money and time on all of this. I was dedicated. I did learn some things about flying, however, and had some interesting experiences.

Toronto has two airports: the big one, Pearson, and the little one, Billy Bishop, which is also called the "island airport." I think Billy Bishop is one of the greatest things I've ever seen. You land right across from the fucking city. Not Queens, not Newark, not Mississauga (where Pearson is). I mean you can walk under a tunnel and be in downtown Toronto. The view is amazing.

Also, you fly on Porter Airlines, which is a small Canadian airline that doesn't fly many places, but it does fly to NYC. The island is so small that only propeller planes can operate there, so the planes are cool. Moreover, they serve you your drink in actual glass glasses, not plastic cups like they do on the other airlines or in kindergarten. The glasses say "Porter" on them. I stole one to take home. Arrest me.

Torontonians complain about their big airport, Pearson. They say it's crowded, that the lines are tremendous, and that it's just a difficult place overall. Torontonians always tell me to fly Porter from the island airport. They say it to me as if it's a treasured secret, a special gift they want to give me, when I complain about all my time flying. "Have you tried Porter?" they offer me, gleefully. "It's so convenient; it's right downtown. Not like that annoying trip to Pearson."

Of course I agree with them that Porter is great. But when they complain about Pearson, it gives me the same feeling I get when I listen to Torontonians complain about the exorbitant cost of their universities.

My son, when we were in Pearson (the "too big and too crowded" airport), stopped me and said, "Dad?" I said, "Yeah?" He said, "Listen." I did, but I didn't hear anything. I said, "What?" And he said, "You can actually hear the people's footsteps, it's so quiet." I laughed, because he had a point.

I looked up the rankings of the worst airports in North America. New York City's three airports – LaGuardia, JFK, and Newark – were ranked the worst three airports on the continent. Pearson ranked something like 46th.

How bad are the NYC airports? Ready? So bad that I find myself in complete agreement with Donald Fucking Trump. That's how bad.

From a *Business Insider* article: "Our airports are like from a third world country," he (Trump) said, calling out LAX and New York City's three international airports: LaGuardia, John F. Kennedy and Newark.

"It's a point many New Yorkers might agree with − in fact, Joe Biden suggested in 2014 that if you blindfolded someone and took them to LaGuardia, they'd think, 'I must be in some third-world country'."[33]

The airports suck so much they can unite me, Joe Biden, and Trump in complete solidarity. To be fair, they are upgrading the terminals. But getting to the airports still sucks. And the delays and cancellations are still awful, among the worst in North America.

Many times I was at the gate, only to be told the flight to New York was delayed. But of all the times I flew, there was a single incident that stood out from all the others. I was at the gate and, typically, they told me there was a ground stop. That means the planes cannot leave the airport due to some delay. But this time the ground delay was coming from Toronto, not New York.

I said to the agent, "I never had a ground delay where the problem was coming from the Toronto side. It's always from the New York side."

He immediately looked at me and said, "Neither have I. I had to check the computer again to make sure I read it correctly."

Anyway, back to that supposedly annoying Pearson airport and the miracle of flying Porter. A few years ago, they built the UP train − an express train that runs from Pearson airport to Union Station, which is the main train station in the heart of downtown Toronto. I LOVE the UP train. Each seat has its own electrical outlet so you can charge your phone or any device. The seats are spacious and comfortable, the people quiet. There are ample luggage compartments everywhere. The conductors are friendly. They sometimes even stop to chat. In fact, I became friendly with one of them because he recognized me from my frequent commuting. The whole trip takes 25 minutes and costs about ten bucks.

---

33 - https://www.businessinsider.com/trump-laguardia-airport-redesign-2016-9

In NYC, the closest airport to Manhattan is LaGuardia. There is no practical, let alone civilized, method of public transportation from LaGuardia to Brooklyn (or Manhattan). You *can* take a packed bus full of loud barbarians shoving each other to get to the subway to Manhattan, a trip that can take 75 minutes and make you want to stop living. As in make you want to just get out of the bus to escape the savages, so you can get relief by falling down on the pavement to drool and die. Anything just to put an end to the misery.

Anyway, at least once a week a Torontonian says to me, "Have you flown out of the island airport? It's so convenient. Not like that terrible trip to Pearson" (The half-hour drive or 25-minute relaxing UP ride).

For the first year of my commuting here I'd agree with them that I loved the island airport and I loved Porter, and that it was nice to have a brief commute to the airport from downtown instead of the half-hour trip from Pearson. But I'd then explain that I live in Brooklyn, and Porter flies to Newark, in New Jersey. Because you have to go through Manhattan, it can take an hour and a half to travel from Newark to Brooklyn in traffic. Also, a taxi ride from Newark to Brooklyn costs more than $100 USD. So, unless I'm traveling straight to Manhattan, and not back home to Brooklyn, Porter isn't useful to me. Yes, on the Toronto side of the trip I can save the 15 minutes going to the island airport instead of going to Pearson on the lovely UP train. But it can add more than an hour and $100 once I land in Newark and have to travel to Brooklyn.

Explaining this is futile, because the response is often the same from Torontonians: "But Porter is so convenient: it's right downtown!"

The first 20 times or so I encountered this response, I tried to explain again to them what it was like once I landed in NYC. I really tried my best to tell them how the trip from Newark to Brooklyn was so awful. But, as I'd explain to them what hell awaits them upon landing in Newark and trying to get to Brooklyn, I'd be met with dazed, vacant looks. Kind of like when you try to point out what's on the TV screen to a dog. Sure enough, they look at where you're pointing, but they can't comprehend what you're talking about. So now when Torontonians offer me the secret miracle solution to all problems – Porter – I just nod and say, "Yeah. It's great." Have a headache? Fly Porter. Owe money on your taxes? Fly Porter. Constipated? Fly Porter.

It's like Torontonians have a learning disability in the area of grasping anything that occurs outside of the Great Toronto area. I've learned to nod and smile when I hear them talk about their unaffordable rents and unaffordable universities, and now I nod and smile when I get the Porter speech. They have no idea what hell confronts a person upon landing in New York City. Oh, how I envy them, those lucky bastards.

While I was flying back and forth between New York and Toronto during these two years, there was a period of about a month when I went on a few dates with a woman in NYC. She was, like me, a psychologist. She's a lovely person, but it didn't work out.

I'm writing about her because one of our conversations crystalizes an important difference between Toronto and New York City. I don't think many Torontonians are fully aware of it, however.

I was telling her how much I liked Toronto, and I sent her some links about Toronto's strengths. One was "9 Reasons to Leave New York for Toronto," from the Huffington Post (10/22/16):

Among the nine reasons were:

"Live in an amazing apartment for half what you're paying now."

"Say goodbye to your commute."

"You can afford to go out more."

I told her how I found a lovely apartment (albeit somewhat small) in the heart of downtown, with a large and private outdoor deck. I didn't have to live in an unrenovated apartment an hour's commute from the city center like I did for a decade in NYC. Within 15 minutes I could be at work; I could even walk to work if I wanted to. And it was all, for me, affordable. Toronto rents have exploded in the last several years and the people are shell-shocked. Even in my two years here I've seen the prices go up substantially. However, even as of now, Toronto rents still amount to less than half of NYC rents. When I first got to Toronto, from my perspective, I was thrilled. It was like "free housing!"

When I showed her these advantages of Toronto, she replied:

"But I have a lot of that in NYC already! Nice apartment, gym, pool, doorman. No commute to work. So I mostly avoid those negative NY things. I do appreciate the art and theater here and go out regularly to events, so I enjoy that part too. A bit sick of too many rich youngsters, haha. Toronto sounds lovely though."

I replied: "That's true, you're very fortunate. New York is much more livable if you have enough money. But many people don't."

She responded, "Yes, that's true: it's a very expensive city to live in and I need Bridgehampton to escape to nature every weekend (where she had her summer house in the Hamptons, of course). Otherwise I might leave too."

We were both psychologists in private practice, probably with similar incomes. The difference was that I'd married and split from a NYC public school teacher, while she'd married and divorced an affluent tax attorney. And that's why she wouldn't benefit from moving to Toronto.

But, for many people, Toronto can provide things NYC can give only to the relatively privileged. And that's one thing that makes me like Toronto a lot on both a personal and political level. Toronto is getting less affordable and it's changing. But for those coming from NYC, without privilege, Toronto is a dream come true. I appreciate it in a way that Torontonians, as well as wealthy New Yorkers – two groups that, for different reasons, don't understand what it's like to struggle with NYC rent – cannot grasp. I love it in Toronto. And I respect the quality of life that Toronto can provide to a much greater percentage of its people than NYC ever could – people like me.

***

Many Torontonians are in awe of New York City. Or, at the least, many like it an awful lot. This manifests itself very clearly on dating sites. I can't tell you the number of times women have written to me saying,

"Why would you ever leave New York for Toronto?" I'm fascinated by this, because the question, so repeatedly uttered, demonstrates a negative view, or at least an inferiority complex, among Torontonians regarding New York. By contrast, I can't imagine a New Yorker asking a Torontonian, "Why would you ever want to leave Toronto for New York City?" It just wouldn't happen.

This isn't universally true, of course. Some Torontonians say they like New York but couldn't live there because it's too intense for them. And some know just about nothing about New York City. One of my clients in Toronto had never heard of Queens. But their take on NYC is overwhelmingly positive.

And that client who never heard of Queens? He's also one of those numerous Canadians who regard Americans as ignorant about the world, of course, unlike the worldly Canadians. There is, as I will describe at times throughout this book, a not-always-subtle anti-Americanism among Canadians. But, as a New York American, I get the full treatment. Either I can be regarded as a guy coming from an unevolved country, or I can be regarded as a guy coming from the most sophisticated, worldly city on earth. Sometimes I get treated as both, numerous times throughout the day, causing me a bit of psychological whiplash. It's been a fascinating, if a bit of an exhausting experience.

A Plum at Pearson

I was at Pearson airport in Toronto, heading back to NYC. As usual, I haven't given myself much of a cushion in terms of time. Fastidious people that advise me to give myself hours of extra time annoy me. They can be so righteous in telling me that if I leave myself hours of extra time for each flight, I'll never have to be stressed about missing my flight. I see their point. But when you travel very frequently, that ends up being hundreds of wasted hours sitting around at the airport per year. And really, getting to the airport two hours early for a one-hour flight? Do they take that into account in their advice to me?

I doubt it. And if they do, it's fine if that's still their preference. I won't judge them. All I ask is that they don't judge me back.

I feel similarly about people who are very neat (it may not surprise you that I'm not). If constant cleaning is their lifestyle choice, that's fine. But what if a person is like me, and not especially bothered by mess? Why is it better for me to spend my time cleaning when I could be doing other things with my time, especially since I have a high tolerance for mess? Why is "cleanliness next to godliness?" Why isn't "cleanliness next to stupid?" I can see both sides. But I don't think messy people judge neat people nearly as much as neat people judge messy people. It's similar with morning people and night people (not surprisingly, I'm a night person). Some morning people judge me because I'm still sleeping at 6 a.m. while they are awake and being productive. But I don't think most night people judge morning people for being fast asleep at midnight, while that's the time they are being most focused and productive. Why can't people see other people's perspectives more easily?

As I write this, I've noticed the theme of relativity is emerging again. I can get frustrated and annoyed with people who can't conceive of how other people do things as being different, but not "less than," the way they like to do things.

Anyway, I digress. As I was saying, I was at Pearson airport and didn't have much of a cushion of time to make my plane. I decided to try to eat healthily and take some fruit to eat on the plane: a plum.

I have Nexus. Nexus is this card that allows you to speed through customs quickly by using a machine where you answer a few questions. The machine then prints out a piece of paper which you wave at the customs officer before proceeding to your gate.

"Am I bringing "$10,000 into the United States?" No. "Am I bringing food into the United States?" I thought for a millisecond about the plastic bag with my plum in it. Then I thought to myself, "I'm obsessing; I'm not bringing food into the United States. That question is for people bringing a significant quantity of food into the United States. I'm just eating a plum on the plane." I checked no.

Big Mistake. I had no idea what awaited me. I sped through, waved my paper at the officer, and started to walk briskly to my gate.

"Hold on, sir!" he said.

I stopped immediately.

"Are you bringing food into the United States?"

"No," I answered. I felt I was being truthful. I don't have the balls and/or stupidity to lie to a security officer's face.

"What's in the bag, sir?" he asked me, sternly.

I said, "It's some fruit to eat on the plane."

He said "Come with me, sir. This is a violation."

I said, "What's the violation?"

He said, "You answered that you were not bringing food into the United States. I gave you another opportunity to correct your answer after you checked 'no' on the machine, and asked you again. And once again you said you were not bringing food into the United States."

"Oh, I'm sorry. I was going to eat the fruit on the plane. I didn't think that counted as 'bringing food into the United States.' I thought that was for a substantial amount of food that was going to be brought into the US."

This was another Big Mistake. In a very authoritarian voice he said, "Let me ask you a question, sir. Is a plum food, sir? Yes or no?"

Okay, now the reality of my situation shot right into me like a lightning bolt. This guy was going to enforce the letter of the law, and also appeared to be thriving on exerting his authority over me. I realized with great clarity that, the more I said, the more trouble I'd be getting myself into. My best option was complete submission.

"Come with me, sir." He then got out of his booth and led me to some hallway I'd never seen. I entered this giant room with a huge desk with like five stations with these officer guys. He said, "Have a seat, sir." I sat and looked at the clock, and worried about missing my flight. I felt like a criminal being held in a police station. I felt terrible. I was scared, confused, and angry.

To make things worse, he then began joking and laughing with the other officers. His mood was completely different. He was having a blast with his buddies. He was definitely taking his time as the minutes before my flight dwindled. After ten minutes of this, I put my hand up, as deferentially and meekly as I could. I finally caught his eye. I said, "I'm sorry, I don't mean to interrupt in any way, but I'm concerned about making my flight." He nodded at me. And then he went on bantering and laughing with his buddies.

Finally, another guard called me up to his station behind the giant desk. He was less militant than my guy. He said, "Let's see ... fruit?" I said, "Yes, I was going to eat a plum on the plane." He said, "Yeah, that's a problem." He filled out a piece of paper and said something like, "That's one violation." I was concerned, but didn't know what that meant, so I asked. Was I in trouble? He said, "If you get three violations, you get your Nexus card taken away."

I made my flight by two minutes.

I was shaken up by that. The next time, I had a wrapped granola bar to eat on the plane. I declared "Yes," to BRINGING FOOD INTO THE UNITED STATES. The guard said, "You checked yes to food. Please go to this room down the hall." I went to this other room (yet another new and unknown giant room in the airport). I waited for about five minutes. The guard said, "What kind of food do you have, sir?" I showed him my wrapped granola bar. He quickly nodded and said, "That's fine." And then I left.

I decided then that nothing good could come from bringing any food to eat on the plane. It's like a situation from a Kafka story. Better to buy food and overpay for it at the gate.

Until ...

One day I forgot I had some food in my coat pocket and checked "no." I didn't end up in jail. Nothing happened.

However, since then I rarely bring anything to eat on the plane. And I will NEVER bring fruit onto a plane. And you better not either.

After a while, I started accumulating little tips and tricks on how to have a better flying experience, such as how to cut corners during the whole process. And also how to not get sick on the plane. For the first six months I was sick all the time. I had the flu for weeks. I'd never been sick that long in my life. A plane is a big germ tube. I learned this painful lesson about germs and planes about two years before most people did when the coronavirus struck. So I decided then to make this list and share it with my friends, and I'm reposting it here. I hope you find it helpful. Now, more than ever, in the age of Covid-19. I can only hope that, by the time you read this, Covid-19 will be a defeated entity, and just the formidable number of germs that existed on planes pre-Covid will remain to be dealt with.

My tips for having a much better flying experience. And not getting sick on the plane.

The day before the flight:
Check in online as soon as possible within 24 hours of the flight, but the rule is you can't check in any less than 90 (sometimes 60) minutes before the flight.

If you do not check in online, they can give your seat away to someone else as much as 90 minutes before an international flight. If you check in online, by contrast, you can get to the gate as late as ten minutes before the flight time (but of course, don't cut it that close).

This way, you don't have to stand in line to check in at the airport, so you can get to the airport a little later if you want.

Also, sometimes they let you pick your seat if you check in online, and if you check in as close to 24 hours in advance, you get a better choice of seats. Avoid the middle seats if possible. Research shows the middle seats are exposed to the most germs from other people (of course, now this has become better-known since Covid).

Take a screenshot of the boarding pass they send you to your phone after you check in online. This way you can just show them the screenshot of your boarding pass instead of having to search your emails on your phone at the airport. It's easier: it's just in your photos this way.

When you show them the boarding pass on your phone, turn your brightness on the phone to maximum. Sometimes they can't read it unless it's really bright.

Consider wearing slip-on shoes without laces to the airport. A lot easier to take on and off.

Bring saline rinse spray for your nose (buy at a pharmacy). Must be 3.4 oz or less. Airplane air is dry and if your nose gets dry you have a much higher chance of getting sick. Wet mucous membranes keep germs from entering the body. Buy a bottle of hand sanitizer. Less than 3.4 oz.

Get LOTS of sleep before the flight. Being sleep-deprived greatly increases our chances of getting sick. This is really important.

Packing hand luggage:

Bring an empty plastic water bottle. After you get through security, fill it with water from a water fountain so you can have it on the plane, for free, instead of paying $4 for a bottle. Unlike carrying plums, I have never been threatened with police action for having an empty water bottle.

Bring two external batteries for your phone. Phones run out of power quickly. And – very important – bring charging cables for your phone and for your batteries. Batteries use Android charging cables for Android phones. iPhone cables for iPhone, of course. Important – bring a block power adapter to connect the USB cable to plug into the electric socket.

Here's an amazing thing. A company called Anker sells a combined charger and external battery in one. With it, you can charge your phone from an electrical outlet and, if there's no outlet, you can charge your iPhone twice from just the battery. First it charges your phone, then the external battery. You can buy it online. It costs around $30, and it's wonderful.

Bring an eye mask to help you sleep.

And an inflatable pillow.

Headphones – wireless is more comfortable, because you won't yank it out of the phone as you twist and turn in your seat.

Dress in layers, so you can take everything off except a t-shirt if the plane is hot – and you can always add clothes if you're cold. They control the temperature, but you can take countermeasures to adjust to it.

Bring a smaller bag for under the seat (backpack, etc.) Put the stuff you'll need during the flight in that. If taking a small carry-on suitcase, put stuff you don't need during the flight in it.

Also, don't pack prescription medications in your checked bag, in case it's lost. You probably know all this already, but just a reminder.

Carry your passport on your person (pockets best) ALL the time. Keep it in the exact same place 100 percent of the time so you can't misplace it and always know where it is.

Do not take fruit or any unpackaged food goods with you. Only buy fruit and unpackaged food if you want them after going through security. When arriving at the destination airport, if it is international, they will only make you throw it out, and you could get in real trouble. They worry about fruit and other unopened foods contaminating their country. Don't say I didn't warn you. I know I have been repeating myself about fruits on planes, but instead of complaining about my being repetitive, you should be thanking me. I'm only looking out for your own good.

On the way to the airport:

Place keys, coins, anything that could go in pockets in a bag, carry-on bag, or just a plastic bag. This way you don't have to waste time and effort at security emptying your pockets and then putting all that stuff back in your pockets. Make sure ALL of your pockets are 100 percent empty before going through security or they'll stop you.

Unless your belt buckle is huge, your belt won't set off the alarm, so you don't have to take it off during security. The worst that could happen is that they'll ask you to take it off.

While waiting at the gate before boarding the plane:

If you check in online, and you should, you still often have to go to the staff at the gate as soon as you get there (before they call anyone to start boarding) and show your passport and boarding pass to them because they check your documents. If you don't check in online (and it's stupid not to) you don't have to do this.

Don't wait until they call your zone or group to board the plane. Get in line one or two zone/groups earlier (excluding zone 1 or 2, which is usually first class or business class). By the time you get to the staff desk, they'll probably have called your zone/group but you'll have a head start over everyone else in your group who sat there obediently waiting for their group to be called. If they haven't called your zone, it doesn't matter, because I've never seen them check anyway. The advantage of this is you'll get to place your carry-on luggage in the bin above before other passengers take up all the storage space.

I realize that, by not waiting obediently until your zone is called, you wouldn't be acting stereotypically Canadian. Therefore, this is a cultural and logistical choice. In this instance, I'm going the New Yorker route, but we each have to do what feels right for us, eh?

(Canadians know what I just wrote, while some New Yorkers may think I just wrote "eh" as in "meh," or so-so. As in someone asking, "Did you like the movie?" And the person answers, "So-so. It was eh." This isn't what I meant. I meant "eh" in the Canadian way.)

While on the plane:

As soon as they close the door and finish boarding, look around the plane to see if there's a better seat (like one without anyone next to you, more legroom, etc.) or whatever other reason you like it better, then nicely ask to move to that seat. The worst that could happen is they tell you no, but they've always told me yes. But don't forget your stuff in the overhead bin when you exit the plane if it's in the bin above your original seat! Don't forget to move all the stuff you had with you in your original seat, seat pocket, etc.

Despite what they say, you can continue using your phone with reception (not in airplane mode) because they never check. Just turn the sound off on your phone so they don't notice. I then put my phone into airplane mode right before take off, because it saves power on the phone and they say it's safer. Although I once sat next to an off-duty flight attendant who told me that was nonsense.

To reduce the chances of getting sick:

Of the eight months I had been traveling, I was sick five of the eight months. I'm the opposite of a germaphobe, but I decided I was going to do everything I could to protect myself. Since doing all this stuff below, I've not gotten sick.

Use lots of hand sanitizer all the time, especially at boarding time, but during the flight also. Wash your hands with soap well, for like 30 seconds, in airport bathrooms before going to the gate to board, and again as soon as you get off the plane after landing. I wrote this advice two years before Covid.

Don't wash your hands on the plane. Airplane bathroom water can contain fecal matter. Use hand sanitizer instead after going to the bathroom.

If you have cleaning wipes, wipe down your tray table before using it.

Don't touch handrails on escalators or moving sidewalks, etc. (germs).

Don't touch the airflow knob above you without a tissue or something, because of germs.

Drink LOTS of water so you don't get dehydrated, and it also lowers your chances of getting sick.

Breathe slowly, with long deep slow breaths, and relax your body and mind throughout the whole airport process. Traveling is stressful even if you don't notice you are stressed. And stress increases the chance of getting sick. Remind yourself to slow down, breathe slowly, and take it easy.

Try to sleep on the plane.

***

Back on the Ground

A New Yorker in Toronto

I'm standing at an intersection in downtown Toronto. The sign is red and says "don't walk." The cars are going in both directions. After a minute, the cars stop and there's no traffic. My body instinctively starts to jerk a bit as I move into action. Then I notice I'm the only one moving. All the other pedestrians remain standing still. I take a second look; there are definitely no cars coming.

I think to myself, "I'm not standing here for no reason." I cross the street against the light. I'm now across the intersection. I look back, and all the people are still standing there.

"Schmucks," I think.

This kind of behavior is why I think even if Canada had the same population as the United States, it would still be a middle power, and not a superpower. I think it's why they never broke from England until 1867. It's also why I feel safer here than in the United States in 2020. However, I have every intention of using my New Yorker edge to my advantage here.

How do you get fifty Canadians out of the pool at once?

Say "Canadians, please get out of the pool."

In Defense of Canadian "Niceness"

In case some readers are feeling I'm being too critical of Canada, I want to make the positive side of the Canadian character clear. I've gotten some feedback that my portrayal of Canadians is stereotypical. I've found, overall, Canada to be a nice, good country and yet a little passive, relative to the United States. I understand I'm not saying anything terribly original about Canadians.

I really can't come up with some Canadian characteristics that Americans would find deeply surprising. There can be something a little bland about Canada compared with the United States. Certainly, compared with New York. I've learned that Canadians don't like my saying this. I don't mean to upset anyone, and I'm sorry if I did.

Of course, my take on Canada isn't universally true – how could it be? There are passive people in any country, including the United States, and there are mean people in Canada, and so on. When I talk about any place and its people, I'm only talking in vague generalities.

But here's my main point. I like Canada, and the biggest reason for this is because it's a good and kind place. Personally, I think that's an extremely positive view.

There's even some psychological research to support my belief that Canadians are a good people overall. I read about a study in which researchers left stamped, unmailed envelopes for strangers[34].

The project examined the number of people who found the letter and would bring it to the mailbox and mail it. In other words, how many people would help other people, just because they could. The study researched Americans and Canadians both pre- and post-9/11.

What they found was illuminating and disturbing. Before 9/11, there was no significant difference in helping behavior between Americans and Canadians. But, after 9/11, Americans had become less helpful to each other, and Canadians had remained equally helpful.

Another fascinating study, reported by the CBC in November 2018,[35] found significant differences in how Americans and Canadians speak, at least on Twitter.

They found that Canadians tended to use more positive words on Twitter. They also found there was some truth to the national stereotypes of Canadians being "nicer" than Americans, based on the words they used online. For example, Canadians tended to more often use the words "great," "amazing," and "good." Americans, by contrast, tended to use more negative and assertive words, such as "hate" and "hurt," and used lots of slang and net-speak.

Moreover, Americans use emojis more often (like smiley faces or faces crying), while Canadians tended to use punctuation and spell out smiley faces. And, when they do use emojis, Canadians' emojis were more often positive, such as a heart.

These studies support my view that, overall, American society is becoming a meaner, pettier place, while Canada is truly kinder.

Throughout this book, I describe various stories where Canadians helped me in ways that deeply touched my heart. Since I was a little boy, I was always upset when people didn't treat each other with

---

34 - "Nicer Up North: Canadians Top Americans in Altruism," *Live Science*, August 24, 2016.

35 - https://www.cbc.ca/news/canada/hamilton/
mcmaster-linguistics-twitter-u-s-canada-trump-1.4915955

kindness. But it works the other way. Seeing people treat each other with kindness and respect is something of a dream come true for me. Of course, I've seen people act like assholes in Canada and saints in New York. I'm talking about overall trends.

One thing I discovered in Canada after a few months here is that this kindness is more apparent on the level of stranger to stranger, or acquaintance to acquaintance. As I began to get to know particular individuals in more depth, I was initially shocked to learn when some of them transitioned from being kind to me to reacting with the pettiness and meanness that I was used to in New York. It wasn't that Canadians were worse than Americans; it was because they acted kinder to me in general, I was surprised when I discovered they're no kinder once you get to know them in depth.

I see some support for this in the study that compared how Canadians and Americans differ in their use of language on Twitter I discussed earlier. As described, the researchers found Canadians were less assertive, more positive, and nicer than Americans in their use of language. However, they interpreted these results as not necessarily meaning Canadians actually were kinder, but that their self-definition of themselves is as a nicer people. That is, because they see themselves as a nicer people, they talk in nicer ways to each other, but not that deep down they are kinder.

My experience is somewhere in the middle. In my opinion, Canadians are nicer to each other than Americans are to each other. Perhaps that's manifested in that they are more polite and speak more respectfully to each other. As the relationships deepen, however, the difference in kindness between the two peoples diminishes.

When I ponder all this, it reminds me of a big lake frozen in the winter. The ice could be broad, covering the entire surface of the lake, and you may feel you can easily walk across the entire lake. However, the ice may not go very deep. Imagine your surprise when you expect the widespread ice to support you, only to find yourself suddenly plunging into the water as the thin ice suddenly disintegrates, even though you were expecting its continued support.

Therefore, I've found the famous Canadian niceness is real, but not very deep. But I think this is still pretty impressive, when one realizes that much of society doesn't take place in more intense personal and professional relationships, but in how people treat each other in general, as acquaintances. How people treat their fellow citizens is extremely important. How I was treated at the airport, when all these strangers waved me ahead of them on the security line, was a particularly Canadian experience for me. People are alike all over, but some societies tend to be kinder than others.

I think I'm giving Canada and its people the biggest compliment of all. It's generally a kind and good place. In my life I've learned, the hard way, over 56 years, that kindness is the most important quality in human relationships. Canada takes the prize on what I consider the best human trait: kindness. As Barack Obama said, "The World needs more Canada".[36]

Canada may come up short on other things compared with some other places, such as initiative or boldness. But you know what? Kindness can sometimes be much more important than initiative and boldness. After all, Nazi Germany once led the world on initiative and boldness.

Canadians – listen up. I feel very lucky your country was there for me.

***

I've been contemplating this whole process and I had a thought which seems quite ironic. What occurred to me was that my whole goal of becoming Canadian is very American of me. Let me explain.

I know this is painting in very broad strokes, and I'm generalizing like crazy. But in the aggregate, it does seem to me, as I described previously, that Canadians are more orderly, more passive, more compliant,

36 - *National Post*, June 29, 2016.

less disruptive, and more willing to go along with "the system" as good citizens than Americans. Americans are more dynamic, more chaotic, more active (as opposed to passive), more violent, more independent-minded, and more individualistic.

So, what does this have to do with me? Well, I'm breaking away from my mother country. And it's "an independent stand that I am compelled to take," as Jefferson would phrase it. Remember that's the reason he gave for writing the Declaration of Independence (to justify that independent stand against Great Britain). And while it's been done before, what I'm doing is quite rare and independent-minded. While so many Americans swamped the Canadian immigration website the day after Trump was elected, and many people said they were going to move to Canada, only a relative handful actually had the balls to make it happen. Most passively resigned themselves to life under Trump. But not me. So what I'm doing is more independent, more active, more chaotic, and more disruptive (I certainly turned my life upside down) than most. In short, this whole book is about my taking a more independent stand. An American stand.

And why am I doing it? Because I, like the people in the colonies, don't like the way I'm being governed. The colonists thought they were being governed by incompetents that didn't care about their interests. I, too, believe I'm being governed by incompetents – Trump and the people that support him. America began as an experiment in how to live a different and higher quality of life, with more autonomy. And that's why I'm doing what I'm doing. I'm becoming Canadian so I can have a more sane and higher quality of life.

And yet I'm also remaining American not only in spirit, but in citizenship as well. I'm glad to be in Canada, and I'm glad I'm still American as well as Canadian. It's who I am now, and it was an independent stand I was compelled to take.

5
How You Can Become Canadian Too - Maybe

This following section is divided into two parts. I wrote part one. It's primarily my description of many of the requirements on a technical basis, of what I needed to provide to meet the demands to become a Canadian permanent resident in my case. However, I'm not an immigration attorney or other expert in Canadian immigration law, so please don't consider my statements on such things to be fully and completely accurate. I just did my best.

To address this concern, the second part was written by Gagan Mandra, who's a Canadian immigration attorney. She's part of the immigration law firm of Nachman, Phulwani, Zimovcak (NPZ) Law Group, P.C. NPZ specializes in United States and Canadian immigration. I asked NPZ to write an overview of the different paths the government of Canada provides for people to become Canadian. This includes Express Entry, which is the path I chose, but it also describes others.

Part One.

I am going to describe many of the bureaucratic requirements – the procedures, documents, etc. – I had to provide to the government to become a Canadian permanent resident. I imagine that you will have to provide many similar things, but again, everyone is a different case, so I can't say that everything will be exactly the same for you, although it may be similar. I can tell you, however, that I believe this should give you a good idea of what to expect overall.

One important thing I should point out is that in my case, I had to acquire one year of Canadian work experience to accumulate enough points under the Canadian Express Entry program. However, you may not need to do that. Points are given for various criteria. Some of these include education, language speaking ability, and age. The younger you are, the more points you get. I'm pretty sure, if I was 25 instead of 56, I wouldn't have needed to get the one year of Canadian work experience, which was so incredibly consuming in terms of time and money. It's quite possible your journey to become Canadian will therefore be easier than mine. **It's imperative you consult with an immigration attorney, or other qualified immigration representative,** or otherwise research what your requirements will be in your unique circumstances to know what you will need to do to become Canadian.

Now I want to explain the differences between having a Canadian work visa, being a Canadian permanent resident, and being a Canadian citizen. Let me start by clarifying the end goal, becoming a Canadian citizen. To become a Canadian citizen you must first become a Canadian permanent resident. The process is similar to the procedure in the United States—you must first get a green card, and then work toward citizenship.

Having a work visa means pretty much that. You can work and live in Canada. However, you can only stay in Canada as long as you have a specific job. And not just any job. You must have a Canadian employer hire you and your work visa is only valid while you're employed by that one specific employer. If you lose this job, you must leave Canada.

By contrast, as a permanent resident, you can do most of what any Canadian citizen can do. For example, you can remain in Canada for the rest of your life, whether you have a job or not. You can own a business of your own. You can receive Canadian health insurance. Some differences, as I understand it, are that only citizens, not permanent residents, can vote or hold high national security office. You must live in Canada 730 days over a five-year period, or you will lose your permanent resident status, which also must be renewed from time to time.

To go from being a permanent resident to a Canadian citizen, you must live in Canada for three out of the last five years, file taxes, be able to prove your ability to speak English and/or French, and pass a test on your knowledge of Canada and your rights, and responsibilities as a Canadian.

As I understand it, practically speaking, you can retain your American and Canadian citizenship simultaneously; you don't have to give one up. But consult your lawyer for the details and nuances of this.

The process to become a Canadian permanent resident is breathtaking, in my opinion, and not in a good way. I can say without exaggeration the whole process was by far the most bureaucratic and arduous experience I've ever had in my entire life. Of course, if you were born an American like me, you probably don't know how difficult the procedure to become an American is. Especially so these days, what with it being post 9/11 and with Trump in office. However, if you're thinking of moving to Canada, please be aware of the magnitude of the bureaucracy which awaits you.

For two years, my life was filled with annoying procedures. Now, remember I had to acquire one year of work experience, so that extended my process by a year. If you don't need to acquire that, and many of you won't, the process could take significantly less time. However, you should also remember that I went through the particular process called Express Entry, which is a common process, ostensibly designed to facilitate, well, express entry. But in my experience, and in the experience of the writer of *The Globe and Mail* op-ed I described earlier, the government can act like "Express Entry" is more like "Slow-Motion Entry." It would take them months to process basic paperwork, and I'd just wait and wait, having no idea what or when things would move along. As an example, the government had notified me I'd met all the requirements for permanent resident status, and they just had to send me a piece of paper to document it. My lawyer told me it usually took about ten days, but it took many more weeks than that. The process was agonizingly slow.

On the other hand, I ran into some Uber drivers who told me it took them only a couple of months to complete the application to get their permanent resident status. My guess is that the length of the process varies with your circumstances, among other factors.

The only other time I remember my life being consumed with paperwork and procedures was when I bought my apartment in New York City. For months I was involved with real estate attorneys, filling out various forms, getting appraisals, contract signings, applying for a mortgage, blah blah blah. But that time period was measured in months, while the Canadian PR process took me years.

As I reviewed my emails to my immigration attorney, reading over our correspondence and the paperwork requirements asked of me over the past couple of years, I started experiencing PTSD-type flashbacks. Well, not literally. But I'm honestly distressed by again facing the details of what I had to go through. My stomach began tightening and my skin became clammy as I was reminded of them one by one.

Here is a long list of much of the documentation I had to provide and procedures I had to follow. I advise you to skim it so you don't lose your mind. Unless your personality is the opposite of mine, and you're a detail-oriented person who thrives on the order of following procedures in a precise manner. Then by all means, enjoy yourself!

Required Documentation:

2013, 2014, 2015, 2016, 2017 US tax returns

Canadian tax returns

A list of countries I visited over the last ten years. Not only that, but they needed the exact dates of my international travel. I had to check my emails over the past decade to try to find the exact dates of leaving and returning. I looked up plane tickets, hotel dates, etc., from a decade ago. Jeez, I didn't even have the same email address ten years ago. All vacations, etc. – the exact dates.

A list of every place I stayed in Canada since I began the application process. When I told my lawyers that I'd stayed in about 50 different Airbnbs over that time, and this request was almost undoable, they wrote something on my behalf to the government and I crossed my fingers. I provided a list of the places I'd stayed in for any substantial length of time, and I explained I'd stayed in many different Airbnbs for only a few days at a time as well. I worried this would sink me, but I got through that.

Copies of birth certificates

Copies of passports

Places of employment I'd worked at in the United States, and dates

Pay stubs from these places

A clearance from the FBI stating I had no history of arrests

A clearance from the FBI stating my *ex-wife* had no history of arrests (well, not my 'ex-wife' technically)

Let me explain. For various reasons my ex-wife and I never legally divorced. However, we've lived in separate apartments and led completely separate lives for about ten years, as we split up in 2010. My attorneys told me – only about a week before the deadline – that my ex-wife would have to get her own FBI clearance and her own physical exam. Even though there was never any intention of her coming to Canada with me. When my lawyers gave me (and therefore my ex) only one week's notice to get this done, you know what I told them? I told them if I asked her for that there'd no longer be a need for an immigration lawyer. We'd need a criminal defense attorney instead, because a homicide against me would ensue.

My attorneys drafted a letter to the Canadian government outlining that we'd lived apart for a decade and she wasn't emigrating to Canada. Of course, the government simply responded, many many weeks later, stating they nevertheless required her FBI clearance and medical exam.

They also wanted a copy of my marriage license.

I paid for her FBI clearance and medical exam, of course. Each individual medical exam is about $500. I had to get one for myself, my son, and my ex-wife. You'll have to get a medical exam too, for whomever the government requires.

The FBI clearance was a ridiculous procedure in which they first tell you how you can get it from the FBI directly – a process so laborious and confusing that an entire industry has sprung up to facilitate processing the forms for an additional fee. You have to make an appointment with these companies. I made the appointment, cancelled my patients to go the appointment, and sat for hours past my appointment time. Finally I knocked on the door to their office and urged them to process me. They seemed completely unaware I was there even though I'd checked in with their receptionist.

Moving on, I also had to undergo:

A language test. As I mentioned in the previous section, you must take a language test (English and/or French) to become Canadian. Again, it doesn't matter if you were born and raised in England or France. You have to register in advance and then take the test. Mine was, as I said, three hours of boredom. And of course, the test costs money. What a racket. There are two companies that provide these tests. One is called CELPIP and the other test is called IELTS. Enjoy.

An ECA (Educational Credential Assessment). This one's a doozy. Fortunately, you may not need to do this, but then again you might, depending on your situation. Because I applied as a "skilled worker," I had to document that I was indeed a fully credentialed psychologist. So I had to send my documents to a company called World Education Services (WES). I believe there are other companies that do this credentialing as well. They all charge a significant fee (of course) and it takes time to get the results. I had to do things like have my university send my transcripts from 1995 to them.

A copy of my PhD diploma. I went to Fordham University, which is a Jesuit school, and the diploma was in Latin. I had to pay another company a fee (of course) to translate my diploma from Latin into English.

I have to point something out about these requests for my professional credentials, because it's such a good example of the system being designed by bureaucrats for bureaucrats, instead of for efficiency. In my situation, as you may recall, I had to acquire one year of Canadian work experience before I could even apply for permanent residency. Therefore, to work as a psychologist in Canada, I had to first become credentialed as a psychologist in Ontario. This credentialing process by itself took about a year. I described this earlier in the book (the supervisor with the challenged memory ...).

To summarize, I'd spent a year meeting all the requirements of the College of Psychologists of Ontario, the regulating body for the profession of psychology in Ontario. I fulfilled all the requirements and began working in Toronto as a psychologist. And then I had to work for a year before I could even start to apply for Canadian permanent residency.

All of this made no difference to the Canadian immigration agency. The Canadian government required me to go through all of these procedures to prove once again I was indeed a credentialed psychologist. I had to pay the WES to gather the records again and wait for them to process and approve them. Even though I was fully approved, registered, and working in Canada as a psychologist for more than a year. God forbid one branch of the Canadian bureaucracy could actually communicate with another branch.

Indeed, the whole process seems designed for the benefit and ease of the bureaucracy and the companies that thrive off it. There's money to be made in the $500 physical exams that take ten minutes, and more money to be made in the duplication of agencies that check your professional credentials, etc. It also seems that no thought or effort was put into how to streamline the process or make it less Kafkaesque for the applicants.

The people that suffer from the process are the people like you and me – the non-Canadians, trying to become Canadian permanent residents. And you know what? We cannot vote. No politician will gain a single vote, or lose a single vote, if they fix the process. Therefore there is no incentive for them to make the process less painful and more efficient. This point was articulated in a Globe and Mail op-ed about the ridiculous rigidity of the Canadian immigration system.[37]

While this may not hurt a politician, it sure does hurt the applicants. But another important point, in my view, is that it also hurts Canada. And because it hurts Canada, the Canadian government should repair their immigration system, for their own sake. Here's why.

Canada is, in geographic size, the second largest country in the world, after Russia. It's larger than the United States. Yet Canada only has a population of 37 million people, about the same population as Poland. In fact, the single state of California has more people than all of Canada. Moreover, California by itself has a significantly larger Gross Domestic Product (GDP) than Canada. Canada needs people. And even more importantly, Canada needs qualified, skilled, and educated people to immigrate there if it wants to thrive, economically and socially.

(Fun fact: Although Canada is indeed slightly larger than the United States, if you count only the land – not bodies of water – the United States has more land. For example, Canada has this huge bay, Hudson Bay, which is 850 miles long. By comparison, Lake Superior, the biggest of the Great Lakes, is only 350 miles long. Even more impressive, Canada has more lakes than the rest of the world combined.)

According to an op-ed in the *The Globe and Mail*, population growth in Canada has fallen by more than half since the 1950s. Moreover, its population is rapidly aging. By the way, this op-ed was an excellent piece which resonates with many of the points in this book about the stupidity and counterproductive rigidity of the Canadian immigration system.

I'm convinced that many people, perhaps most, are deterred from pursuing or completing the application process to become Canadian

37 - (Behind paywall) https://www.theglobeandmail.com/opinion/article-harry-and-meghan-have-no-idea-immigrating-to-canada-is-hard/

because it's so arduous, lengthy, and expensive. I'm not bragging, but I'm pretty sure my level of dedication and commitment to becoming Canadian was unusually high, and that's one major reason I was successful. If the government want to promote the well-being of Canada, they should overhaul their immigration process system. It's your choice, Canada. It would be nice if you were kind enough to reform your process on behalf of us, the applicants. But I urge you to streamline your process for your own benefit. If you won't do it for us, Canada, do it for you.

Choosing an Immigration Attorney

I hope I've made it clear that, in my opinion, the application process to become a Canadian permanent resident can be difficult, confusing, complicated, and burdensome (if you don't get that by now, you're an idiot). Therefore I recommend you hire a Canadian immigration attorney to help you through the process. If I'd not hired an immigration attorney, I wouldn't have understood and successfully managed the process. Perhaps, just perhaps, if your situation is much simpler than mine you may not need one, but I'm not even sure about that. Therefore my advice is for everyone to hire an immigration attorney.

Don't just hire any immigration attorney, however. Choosing a good immigration attorney is essential. My first immigration attorney was awful. She had a good website and actually came recommended by another attorney. She was friendly and accessible – before I gave her my money. But she explained the immigration process to me in a way I found confusing. When I would call her up to seek clarification, it was very difficult to get her on the phone. Finally, when she did find the time to talk to me, I continued to experience her explanations as unclear and confounding. And I'm no dummy; I have a PhD. I actually went on a date with another Torontonian immigration attorney who told me this lawyer was very good at marketing herself but wasn't a good attorney. That seemed about right.

My future employer recommended a different immigration law firm, and this one was more professional and better at communicating. They knew the rules and procedures backwards and forwards. It was a big improvement.

However, although they described themselves as a "boutique" firm, I didn't experience them that way. Much like the Canadian government, they seemed often (not always, but sometimes) more concerned with their own comfort and convenience than mine. For example, I'd been flying back and forth between Toronto and New York, at great cost in time and money, as I described earlier. I basically went broke in the process. It was only after I completed the year of employment that we began focusing on my other requirements – such as the language test and the psychologist accreditation process. If they'd paid a bit more attention to my particular needs and focused on what I could do to expedite the already-too-lengthy process, it would've saved me thousands and thousands of dollars and many months.

To be fair, I did find an email where they urged me to take care of these things early, but among the more than 100 emails, I'm aware of this single instance, and it was never said in conversation to the best of my memory – even though they were fully aware I was traveling back and forth at great expense each month. Had they just spent a few minutes thinking about my particular needs and life situation and how to make things easier for me, it would've made a huge difference in my life. But their focus was on just making sure the government requirements were followed, which is good – but it certainly wasn't a "custom-fit" for my needs. There was nothing boutique about this. They frequently didn't give me a sufficient heads-up about upcoming deadlines. As I mentioned previously, they didn't let me know my ex-wife would need to get an FBI clearance and medical until about a week before it was due. They only gave me several days to complete a complex online government form because they were closing their office for their holiday weekend. At another time they told me they needed medical results by noon, because they were heading into another three-day holiday weekend and wanted to leave early. I got the message that sometimes their convenience, not my interests, was their priority. Not always, to be fair to them. Sometimes they went above and beyond in their efforts, such as giving me their cell number in case I ran into a problem with officials at the airport on a Saturday. I guess it was hit or miss with them. But they were very competent and knew their stuff, and without their expertise I wouldn't have been able to successfully complete the process.

So what's the take-away from all of this for you, dear reader? My advice is:

1. Hire an immigration attorney; don't do it yourself.

2. Hire a Canadian one, because American immigration attorneys don't know about Canadian immigration procedures.

3. Choose your immigration attorney carefully. Try to get personal recommendations. Try to avoid just trusting a well-designed website, if possible. Interview the attorney. See if they're responsive to your questions and explain things clearly. Ask yourself if you feel comfortable talking to them. And they probably will ask for a retainer. If you find yourself working with them and you're not satisfied, leave them. You may lose some of your retainer, which sucks. But I've found, like many fields, there's a great variety in the quality of the service depending on the individual provider. Don't be shy about switching attorneys. The process of becoming Canadian is difficult enough; your attorney should help guide you and facilitate the process as much as possible. Good luck.

4. This is a last-minute addendum. I just became aware that there's something called an agent or representative. I cannot really comment, or recommend or not recommend these things (or even know if they are the same thing), but you may want to investigate if these are useful and/or less expensive than an immigration attorney. I found a website[38] which may be helpful, by the Canadian government, as a starting point for your research.

I just want to wish you, dear reader, a smoother and faster journey than mine if you choose to undertake this mission to become Canadian.

---

38 - https://www.canada.ca/en/immigration-refugees-citizenship/services/immigration-citizenship-representative.html

Part Two. - Path to Canadian Citizenship:

Canada's immigration system provides numerous opportunities for individuals to visit Canada temporarily or permanently. Canada continues to introduce new programs and refine the existing ones with the goals of improving economic outcomes of entering immigrants, responding to labor market shortages, and spreading new immigrants evenly across Canada.

Most individuals who successfully apply for permanent residence are chosen through Canada's economic-based immigration programs – Express Entry system and Provincial Nominee Programs ("PNPs"). We discuss these programs in detail below. They are paths to acquire Canadian citizenship.

Canada also offers temporary work permits which allow foreign nationals to enter Canada, gain work experience and then find eligibility under the Express Entry system or PNP for Permanent Residency. These work permits are issued under the Start-up Visa Program, Temporary Foreign Worker Program, International Mobility Program and more. The work permits aren't direct paths for citizenship but are roadmaps for foreign nationals to settle in Canada permanently, if they meet the requirements under Express Entry or PNP.

Canada is a premier destination for International students, who make immense cultural and social contributions in the community, and generate CA$21 billion in economic activity. International students are eligible to apply for permanent residency through one of the economic-based programs on completion of their studies.

We discuss below some of the most popular economic and family-based immigration programs to Canada.

Express Entry: The Express Entry system provides a pathway to permanent residence for skilled workers in Canada. Under this system, the government essentially invites potential skilled foreign workers to permanent residency to Canada and those already in Canada, an option to reside as a permanent resident, based on their skill and ability to contribute to the growth of the country. The Express Entry has three economic immigration programs – Federal Skilled Worker Program ("FSWP"), Federal Skilled Trades Program ("FST"), and Canadian Experience Class ("CEC"). The provinces and territories can also recruit candidates from the Express Entry pool through the Provincial Nomination Program (discussed below).

Each of the above immigration programs have different requirements. The Federal Skilled Worker Program requires a Canadian Language Benchmark of seven or more, and Canadian or foreign experience in a management, professional or technical job for one year (continuous) in the last ten years. The Federal Skilled Trades Program requires a Canadian Language Benchmark of five or more, Canadian or foreign experience in technical jobs for two years (continuous) in the last five years, a valid job offer for full time employment for a total period of at least one year, or a "certificate of qualification" issued by the body that governs trades in a Canadian province, territory or by a federal authority. The Canadian Experience Class requires a Canadian Language Benchmark of seven or more if an applicant's occupation is in a management or in a professional field or five, if the applicant's occupation is in a technical field; and Canadian experience in a management, professional or technical job for one year (continuous) in the last three years.

Provincial Nominee Programs: All 13 of Canada's provinces and territories run their own immigration programs. These programs are referred to as Provincial Nominee Programs. The fact that each province and territory is empowered to run the program means they are able to tailor it to reflect the unique needs of their varying populations and economies. The provinces and territories are granted the opportunity to nominate individuals and their families who wish to settle in a particular province or territory.

As the economics and demographics of each province and territory in Canada are unique, each PNP is designed to reflect these differences. Some provinces may wish to prioritize recruiting skilled workers in a certain occupation, and others may prioritize bringing in individuals who are proficient in French. To participate in a PNP, you'll need to first apply to the province for your provincial nomination. Qualifying for the nomination will depend on whether you have the skills and work experience, the education level necessary to settle in Canada and financially support yourself and your family. Also, you must be able to meet the labor market needs of the province and Canada as a whole. The province or territory will need to approve your application.

As PNPs are run by the provinces and territories, but final immigration decisions rest with the federal government, there's a second part to a PNP application. Once approved by a province, you need to submit an additional application to Canada's Federal Government to obtain Canadian Permanent Resident status. You must apply within a specific time. The province will inform you as to whether you must apply through Canada's Express Entry system or through the regular application process. If your PNP requires Express Entry, you'll need to complete an Express Entry profile and be accepted into the Express Entry pool, if you're not already in the pool.

Work Permit: A work permit or authorization to work without a permit is required for a foreign national to be allowed to work in Canada under either of the programs – the Temporary Foreign Worker Program or the International Mobility Program. These are dual intent programs, which are legitimate. Dual intent is present when a foreign national who has applied or may apply for permanent residence in Canada also applies for a temporary period as a worker. The foreign national will gain Canadian work experience and may then be found eligible for permanent residency under the Express Entry system or Provincial Nominee Program.

The term "work" is defined as an activity for which wages are paid or commission is earned or that competes directly with activities of Canadian citizens or permanent residents in the Canadian labor market.

Start-up Visa Program: The entrepreneurs with business ideas and support of Canadian investors can become permanent residents and launch their business in Canada. To qualify for the Start-up Visa Program, you must have a qualifying business where each applicant holds ten per cent or more of the voting rights attached to all shares of the corporation outstanding at that time, and applicants and the designated organizations jointly hold more than 50 per cent of the total voting rights attached to all shares of the corporation outstanding at that time. To elaborate further, your business idea and venture must get the support of one of the three designated organizations – Venture Capital Funds, Angel Investor Groups or Business Incubators.

Each of the organizations has its own intake process for the proposals and criteria to assess the business plans. For example, the Venture Capital Funds require a minimum investment of CAD $200,000, and Angel Investor Groups require a minimum investment of CAD $75,000,000. With Business Incubators, minimum investment isn't required but you must be accepted into a Canadian business incubator program.

Temporary Foreign Workers Program: The employers must obtain a Labor Market Impact Assessment ("LMIA") to hire foreign workers to fill temporary labor and skill shortages. The LMIA verifies there is a need for a temporary worker and that no Canadians or permanent residents are available to do the job.

Regardless of where you apply, you must satisfy an immigration officer you'll leave Canada at the end of your employment; show you have enough money during your stay in Canada to take care of yourself and your family members and to return home; be law-abiding and have no record of criminal activity (you may be asked to provide a Police Clearance Certificate); not be a danger to the security of Canada; be in good health and provide a complete medical examination, if required; not intend to engage in employment with an employer on the list of ineligible employers; and provide an immigration officer with any additional documents they require to prove you can enter the country.

International Mobility Program ("IMP"): The IMP allows employers to hire temporary workers without an LMIA. The exemptions from the

LMIA process are based on the broader economic, cultural or other competitive advantage for Canada and/or reciprocal benefits enjoyed by Canadians and permanent residents.

International Students: Canada is a destination for international students, attributed to strong schools and programs of study in both English and French, welcoming diverse communities with an enviable quality of life and endless opportunities to start a career. Eventually, these students become ideal candidates for permanent residency with their Canadian education, in-demand labor skills, and proficiency in one of the official languages.

In 2018, international students in Canada contributed an estimated CAD $21.6 billion to the country's GDP and supported almost 170,000 jobs for the nation's middle class. This is a significant economic contribution, and one that's felt across the country.

Family-based immigration: A Canadian citizen or a permanent resident can sponsor a spouse, common-law partner or conjugal partner to immigrate to Canada. If you're a Canadian citizen living outside Canada, you must show you plan to live in Canada when the person you want to sponsor becomes a permanent resident. But you cannot sponsor if you're a permanent resident living outside Canada.

In most cases, there's no low-income-cut-off ("LICO") for spouse sponsorships. However, if either a spouse or partner you're sponsoring has a dependent child, you must meet a minimum LICO score, which is determined by the Canadian government each year.

Citizenship by Descent: An individual is likely a Canadian citizen if at least one parent was born in Canada or became a naturalized Canadian citizen before the person was born. Parent is defined as biological parents, or non-biological parents if they are the child's legal parents at the time of birth. The definition doesn't include parents who adopted the child after they were born or are legal guardians to the child.

DISCLAIMER: The above information is provided at the request of the author of this book and it is provided merely for educational purposes and as a general guide to help the reader understand the present state of the Canadian immigration laws. This information isn't to be construed as legal advice for any particular case. No lawyer-client relationship is established. The immigration and nationality laws of Canada are dynamic and complex and it's highly recommended that you consider engaging the services of a qualified Canadian immigration lawyer to analyze the particular facts and circumstances of your matter.

At NPZ, our US and Canadian lawyers help clients with regard to employment and family immigration issues. If you or your friends or family have any questions, please feel free to contact us at info@visa-serve.com, or you can call our offices at 201-670-0006 (x 100). We look forward to being able to assist you.

6

To Justify Myself in the Independent Stand I Was Compelled to Take:

(Or, "Why the Hell Did I Do This?") Part Two:

More Personal Reasons

Father

Now I'd like to step back and add another major reason, beyond those I described previously, to explain why I decided to go to Canada in the first place. It's very personal.

I'm Jewish. Many of my relatives are Holocaust survivors. I believe this is another reason I moved to Canada while others only thought about it.

My father himself was in the Holocaust. His father, my grandfather, was murdered in Auschwitz. I'm named after my grandfather.

My father was born in 1934 and World War II started in 1939, so he was only a five-year-old boy when Germany invaded Poland to start the war. However, the Nazis' moves to restrict the rights of Jews began years before that.

Recall that my parents split when I was six years old. I'd visit my father on Sundays. His mother lived upstairs from him with her brother, my "Uncle Sam." I'd hear my father say in a Yiddish accent "Schmeedt" when he'd address him, so I assume that was his real name, and Sam was the Americanized version. They would all speak in Yiddish. My grandmother, Rachel, never learned to speak English well, even though she ended up spending more than 50 years in the United States. That always bothered me, because I think 50 years is more than enough time to learn the mainstream language of your new country.

She would sit me and my sister down on her sofa for what seemed like unending hours, telling us stories in broken English about people in the "old country," Poland. She'd sit very close to me and focus her eyes on mine. It was an uncanny feeling, like being ensconced in some kind of force field generated by aliens to trap and immobilize Kirk and Spock from *Star Trek*. I never knew, or cared, about any of those people in my grandmother's stories. Not only did I not care, but I couldn't really follow what she was saying anyway because her English was so bad. The only thing I can compare it to was learning Spanish in Ms. Principi's class.

Nevertheless, my grandmother demanded my full attention during those episodes of drudgery. My mind would start to wander almost immediately and I'd look away and daydream. She had, however, an uncanny ability to instantaneously notice this and tell me to look at her and keep listening. How I wish I could've called Scotty to beam me up out of there.

It was agony. She had no sense of narrative arc. I'm sure she was trying to share with me what life was like in Poland, and I wish I could've gained something from her knowledge and experiences. But all I could feel was a sense of my drowning in a sea of pointlessness. It was as if time had collapsed into infinity. I once read a science fiction story where one second of normal time lasted hours for a person who was trapped in a body container and couldn't move. The person went insane as time just stopped and an eternity filled with nothingness awaited him. Yeah, it was kinda like that.

Not that she was a bad person, because she certainly meant no harm. It's just that as she droned on about how she had a friend who had a friend in the old country that owned a store and how their daughter went for a walk and zzzzzzzz ...

However, there was one topic my grandmother, my father, and Sam would talk about that I felt very keenly. They would sit me down at the kitchen table and begin to tell stories about their family experiences in the Holocaust.

The ironic thing is, unlike my grandmother's other stories, these stories never went on for long. In fact, the problem was that these particular stories were never long enough. These tales always stopped short when they would choke up and begin to cry. And then they'd say they didn't want to talk anymore. This is a pattern when people try to talk about trauma.

I don't remember the content of these stories from the kitchen table, unfortunately. I've learned that this forgetting, on my part, and the inability to speak of it on the survivors' part, are typical patterns in families of Holocaust survivors.

I wasn't able to make sense of all this as a boy. But, nevertheless, it had a huge effect on me. As the years went on, I began to form an understanding of what had happened. Something – I didn't know precisely what, but clearly something terrible – had happened to them. In a way, this was even worse than if they'd been able to tell me a complete and coherent story. Because, as a boy, I was left to fill in with my imagination what could've happened. Whatever it was, it was unspeakable. I didn't really imagine anything in particular. I just knew that SOMETHING had happened that was beyond their ability to bear. And the fact I can't remember the content of the stories suggests to me I was unable to bear them as well. Nothing else in my life was like this. Anything else in life could be spoken about. Whatever this thing was, even as a kid I knew this was something terribly different than everything else.

And that hit me very deeply emotionally, even though as a boy I wasn't consciously aware of it. But it vicariously traumatized me.

When I was in my twenties, my father once brought my sister and my half-brother and me to a park in Brooklyn to tell us in detail what had happened to our family in the Holocaust. It was kind of dramatic. I took notes.

I've since lost these notes and, even worse, I barely remember anything from the talk. And that's not all. My father refuses to speak about it again. So now I feel sick that I cannot remember much, and I'm torn between demanding my father speak of it again and risk retraumatizing him on the one hand, and on the other hand the need for me, (and future generations) to know what happened and not have it be lost with him. I do have isolated fragments, a few individual stories that give me just enough to visualize some experiences they went through, but not enough to form a complete picture. For example, my father told me a story that occurred when he was five years old, shortly after his father was taken away. Two German soldiers had entered their home and told them they were seizing it from them and they would be kicked out. My father, terrified, started to cry. One of the German soldiers said to him, "I'll give you something to cry about, Jewboy!" and punched him in the face.

There are a few other stories I remember, but I think you get the point. So I have enough bits of information to know the level of pain involved here.

And so I realize, in a way that most Americans don't really grasp, that awful things can and do happen on this scale. I always knew, even as a boy, that societies can break down and people can do terrible things to each other. Not only on an individual level, like with a murder. I know that one ethnic group can destroy another group, that they can "other" them. They can deem them "less than human" and start wiping them out. And they can be very successful at it, if that's the word.

My point in saying all this is that, early on in life, I was made aware in a very profound way that terrible things can and do happen in the world. For example, on 9/11 I was of course in New York City (because I was always in fucking New York City). I was not shocked that day. The only thing I found surprising was that nothing like this had happened in the United States before. I felt we'd been lucky and protected for so long while mass murder due to terrorism had been happening in other countries for a long time. I remember thinking about how dumb and naive Americans can be. I was in temple and the rabbi was talking about how people had been coming up to him, trying to make sense of 9/11, saying, "Rabbi, how could something like this have happened?" I remember sitting in my seat in synagogue thinking, "What idiots."

Because of all this, I've always had an interest in the world, relative to most Americans. To me, Europe and the rest of the world are not faraway places that have nothing to do with my life and that I don't have to think about. To me, these places are as close as my father's tears.

So, what does this have to do with Canada?

Well, let me be clear. I'm not saying Donald Trump is akin to Adolf Hitler. Almost definitely, whatever negative effect he'll have on the country and the world won't be nearly as bad as what happened in Germany.

But here's my point – it doesn't have to be. It could be one-tenth as bad, and that's still plenty bad.

Germany, like the United States, was a democracy. Hitler didn't seize power in a military coup. The people elected him. And then, once in power, he began to change the country, slowly at first, faster later – and eventually turned it into the Nazi Germany we all know about. This point has been made in many books and articles.

Following their loss in World War I, the German people felt a loss of self-esteem and suffered a national humiliation. Their economy was in bad shape, and there was a lot of anxiety about economic security. Hitler and his followers built upon these apprehensions by primarily blaming one group for their problems: Jews. Some other groups were targeted as well, such as homosexuals, Gypsies, and the disabled. At first their rights were slowly rescinded, but as the years went on the government measures worsened, until Jews and others were removed from their homes and killed by the millions in death camps.

People just love to blame others when times are tough. This problem isn't unique to Nazi Germany, of course; history is replete with many examples in other places and other times.

For example, in the 1990s in Europe, Serbia killed many thousands of Bosnian Muslims in what they called "ethnic cleansing." A few years later the Serbs tried to pull something similar in Kosovo, among other Muslims. I joined a group called "Jews Against Genocide, the New York Committee to Save Bosnia." I'm against genocide, you see, no matter what group is being targeted.

One day we met with a rabbi for a meeting. I remember what he said. He told us that when his congregants ask him if the Serbs' actions against the Bosnians are as bad as the Holocaust, he responded by saying the question was irrelevant. His answer is that it was "bad enough."

You can probably see where I'm going with this. Donald Trump is no Hitler. But when the people of the United States turn to a leader who unfairly blames a group for its problems, and then starts to mistreat that group, I get very worried.

There's strong evidence that immigrants commit crimes at lower rates than Americans who were born in the United States. Yet Trump and his supporters go on and on, citing every example of crimes committed by immigrants. Of course, some immigrants do commit crimes, as does any group, so Trump will always be able to come up with examples. But because he doesn't respect science or logic, the fact that on average these groups are less dangerous than other Americans doesn't matter to him or his followers. If you think about it, based on the evidence, if you really wanted to make the United States safer, you should get rid of everyone who was born here and just let the immigrants remain. Not that I'm advocating that, of course. I'm just pointing out how stupid and how awful Trump and his enablers are.

Frankly, I don't know where all this blaming of immigrants will lead. Once you open that Pandora's box of hate, no one can know in advance how bad it will get. But I'm in agreement with the rabbi's words – it will be bad enough. I'm not, as a white, male, American-born Jew, at the highest risk, for sure – although the Anti-Defamation League noted the sharp increase in anti-semitic crimes in 2018, which included the mass murder at the Pittsburgh Synagogue.[39] But it's not only about the Jews. Like when I fought for the Bosnian Muslims, it's about caring about acts of hate against other groups, regardless of who they are. It's the sick thinking, and the brutal actions, that result from these kinds of beliefs that disturb me.

When I saw the Trump movement growing, alarm bells went off in my psyche.

There is a *The Twilight Zone* episode, written by the show's creator Rod Serling, entitled "He's Alive," which takes place in the United States, in which a punk, by the name of Peter Vollmer, is played by a young Dennis Hopper. Vollmer, who was humiliated and mistreated as a boy, grows up into a guy who attempts to compensate for his underlying insecurity by trying to come across as a strong leader. He starts to lead a neo-Nazi group. He has a lot of difficulty gaining traction, and people just laugh at him.

One day, however, Vollmer is visited by a man in the shadows, who gives him some advice on how to become more effective at gaining followers for his hateful movement. The man tells Vollmer: "Let us start by your learning what are the dynamics of a crowd. How do you move a mob, Mr. Vollmer? How do you excite them? How do you make them feel as one with you?

Join them. When you speak to them, speak to them as if you were a member of the mob. Speak to them in their language, on their level. Make their hate your hate. If they are poor, talk to them of poverty. If they are afraid, talk to them of their fears. And if they are angry, Mr. Vollmer – if they are angry – give them objects for their anger.

"But most of all – the thing that is most of the essence, Mr. Vollmer – is that you make this mob an extension of yourself. Say to them things like, 'They call us hate mongers; they say we're prejudiced. They say we're biased. They say we hate minorities. Minorities. Understand the term, neighbors. Minorities. Should I tell you who are the minorities?

39 - https://www.adl.org/audit2018

Should I tell you? We! We are the minorities!' Start it that way, Mr. Vollmer."

Does any of this sound familiar?

Vollmer takes his advice and starts to be successful, and whips up the crowd. He states:

"Shall I tell you who the minorities are? We are the minorities! Because patriotism is a minority. Because love of country is the minority. Because to live in a free, white America seems to be of a minority opinion!"

Of course, the man in the shadows turns out to be the ghost of Hitler.

Rod Serling ends the episode, as he does all *The Twilight Zone* episodes, with his closing narration:

"He's alive so long as these evils exist. Remember that when he comes to your town. Remember it when you hear his voice speaking out through others. Remember it when you hear a name called, a minority attacked, any blind, unreasoning assault on a people or any human being. He's alive because through these things we keep him alive."

Bret Stephens, a conservative journalist, wrote a column in *The New York Times* on June 5, 2020.[40] In it he discussed why he thought Twitter was Trump's favorite mode of communication. Stephens said Trump's use of the Twitter format was perfectly crafted to antagonize and disparage people. He said Trump's way of speaking was designed to reduce the national discourse to a primitive level of "grunts and counter-grunts." Fair enough. But what really caught my attention was when Stephens wrote this (italics mine): "That's a level that suits Trump because it's the level at which he excels. Anyone who studies Trump's tweets carefully must come away impressed by the way he has mastered the demagogic arts. *He doesn't lead his base, as most politicians do. He personifies it. He speaks to his followers as if he were them. He cultivates their resentments, demonizes their opponents, validates their hatreds.*"

---

40 - https://www.nytimes.com/2020/06/05/opinion/donald-trump.html

Wow. Compare these words from those words from that *The Twilight Zone* episode from 56 years ago. Let me reiterate those words when Hitler was coaching the American in how to succeed in America as a leader of the right-wing hatemongers:

"Join them. When you speak to them, speak to them as if you were a member of the mob. Speak to them in their language, on their level. Make their hate your hate."

Stephens also wrote in his column: "Whatever this has achieved for him (Trump) or them, it's a calamity for us."

Most people in Germany – Jews and others – never thought things were going to get that bad. They stayed in Germany, and they paid for that mistake with their lives. I wasn't going to be like them. I was going to be proactive. And so I wanted to find out what would be involved in my becoming a dual citizen, of Canada and the US. I wanted a plan B. I didn't know in November 2016 if I would move or not. I just knew I had to deal with this catastrophe of Trump being elected by taking some action. I didn't want to quake in fear or only boil in anger, as most of my friends were doing. I wanted to empower myself.

Some of my friends say they wanted to fight, to protest Trump, etc. and I'm 100 percent for that. But I'm not grandiose enough to think that my own individual efforts can change the country enough so that my family and I can be protected. I reasoned that the most powerful thing I could do for myself and my family was to look into getting the hell out. And it wasn't an either/or choice. I would always retain my American citizenship and would continue to protest and oppose Trump and support enlightened positions and policies instead. But why not do both?

And so I did.

Mother

When I was in my late twenties, I was in graduate school and I was struggling financially. Unless you come from privilege, graduate school is a time of poverty. I did, however, have a girlfriend in graduate school who certainly wasn't struggling financially. Her father was a wealthy Manhattan real estate developer (and he actually rebuffed Trump when Trump wanted to be an investor in his luxury condo skyscraper). Anyway, my sister and I had been stupid and gotten ourselves in some credit card debt. Mine was around $10,000.

My maternal grandparents, whom I loved dearly, had recently died. I last saw my grandfather in 1992 when I went to visit him in Florida. He told me he had left instructions in his will that all four of his grandchildren would receive $50,000 each. And remember that, since this was the 1990s, $50,000 was worth significantly more than it is now.

But shortly after that, both my mother and her sister (my aunt) had become single. My mother divorced her first husband, my father, and was now divorcing her second husband. My grandfather decided to change his will because he was worried about his daughters and wanted them to have more discretion over the money. He altered his will so that each of his two daughters would receive the money in full (I believe it was about $400,000 at the time). But he wrote that they should give it to their own children as they saw fit.

My mother saw fit to give me $2,000. I didn't ask for more. Later, however, when I was experiencing financial distress, I asked her to go out to lunch with me. At the lunch I told her that I was having financial difficulties. I said that my sister Cindy and I were both struggling with credit card debt and, if we could get that off our backs, we could have a fresh start and things would get a lot easier for us. I asked her about giving us $10,000 each (enough to pay off the credit card debt), even though I knew that grandpa was originally thinking about $50,000 for us each before my mother divorced.

My mother immediately replied, "Absolutely not." I will always remember how firm her voice was. And so that was that; I knew not to question it. I was silent. But then, after a pause, my mother said:

"You know, Herb Rubenfeld's (our neighbor on Long Island) son Jeffrey was in a car accident. He wasn't really badly hurt, but he collected a lot of money in a settlement. Maybe you should try that."

Some people react to this story by insisting my mother must've been joking. My mother was not joking.

You see, my mother has a Narcissistic Personality Disorder (NPD). This means that my mother has great difficulty seeing and feeling the needs of others, especially if they get in the way of her own needs. It isn't as if she means to hurt others. It's just that, because of her NPD, other people simply exist as objects to either gratify her needs or to deny her those needs. Intellectually, she's sometimes capable of understanding their needs, but she doesn't usually feel them and rarely even thinks about them. It's all about her.

Let me elaborate. If other people give her what she wants – money, admiration, etc. – they are considered "good." If other people fail to give to her, or take from her – they are "bad." The idea that they have their own legitimate needs, which may at times clash with hers, isn't on her radar. All that matters is other people's impact on her.

This story shows my mom in a more positive light than she sometimes was. She actually wanted to help me, albeit by suggesting I get hit by a car. She did show a rudimentary awareness that I had a need separate than hers. And by suggesting I get hit by a car, she was trying to help me get money. As long as she didn't have to sacrifice anything for herself.

My parents divorced when I was six years old. They fought a lot, and there was much rage and chaos in front of me as a young child. As a young boy, I developed a vicious phobia of dogs because of my own anxious and angry feelings.

A few years ago, I gave a talk at a psychology conference. The topic was how being a child of divorce shaped our career choices.

This is drawn from that psychology talk: "After the divorce my younger sister and I lived with my mother in the Riverdale section of the Bronx. We would visit my father on weekends. Every Sunday night, upon returning, my mother would grill me about my father. 'Tell me everything,' she would instruct me. My mother sat me down for a talk. This talk is burned into my brain. 'You know,' she began, 'your father doesn't love you. I'm the only one who really loves you. If your father loved you, he would be giving us more money. You understand that your father doesn't love you, right Stephen?' she said.

"Right," my seven-year-old self would dutifully say, taking this in as an essential truth.

Because of my mother's NPD, she couldn't see – it simply didn't occur to her – that to denigrate my father was hurtful to me. She wasn't thinking it would harm me by telling me when I was a young boy that my father didn't love me. Because she was the only one that psychologically existed, that had emotional needs, I, or anyone for that matter – was just an extension of herself. For her to control her antipathy for my father in front of me would be to understand that I was different from her and had my own separate needs from her. It was beyond her capability to perceive me and sacrifice her needs for mine, because she has a Narcissistic Personality Disorder.

Therefore I grew up thinking my father didn't love me. It wasn't until I was in my twenties that I realized what had happened, after I started therapy. And boy, was I pissed. Because all of this damaged me very much, even though I didn't consciously know it for a long time. I spent a long, long time in therapy repairing myself.

There are many other examples, but I'll give only one more. When I was a boy, my mother told me that while she was married to my father, he had a "nervous breakdown" and was psychiatrically hospitalized for depression. When my mother told me this story, she would emphasize that she was so embarrassed that her husband was in the psychiatric hospital. She told me that when she visited him in the hospital, she would look around when entering and leaving the building, hoping she didn't see anyone she knew so no one would recognize her because she felt so humiliated. My mother never did mention any concern for my father's depression.

So, what does any of this have to do with Canada?

Well, because I was raised with a parent who has NPD, I instinctively know what NPD feels like. Let me put it this way: you know how, if you are exposed to a virus such as Covid-19, your body naturally develops antibodies toward it? The antibodies are made in reaction to the disease, and they stay in your system, ready to recognize and defend you from it the next time you encounter it? Well, that's how it was when I saw Trump. Instinctively, I just knew what he was. The way he perceives people, and patterns of his reactions, were all very familiar to me.

Having NPD is a completely different way of being in the world of people, of existing, than that of normal people. When people say someone's self-absorbed, even "narcissistic," they may think they're talking about the same thing as a person with NPD. They're wrong. It's like saying someone with a headache is experiencing the same thing as a person with a full-blown migraine. It's a whole other order of magnitude.

Trump, like my mother, isn't like most people. It isn't just that he's a selfish guy. It's that he's incapable of understanding that another person can have their own separate needs. He's all that matters; he's all that exists. It isn't that he's selfish really. To be selfish means to be aware of others' needs and decide to put yourself first. It's different than that – you're all that matters. Other people are there, but again, they only exist to you to supply or deny.

Think about it. When Trump likes someone, praises someone, it's usually because they've supported him – with praise, or defended his actions, or given him something else he wants or needs. Similarly, when he attacks someone, it's not because they did something bad for other people. It's because they did something bad for him. It's usually because they opposed him, or denied him something he needs. Their own traits, and personal qualities, are curiously absent from his take on them. Follow the news and see how often this pattern holds up.

Trump's presidency is replete with examples of this. Remember him calling Hillary, his opponent, a "nasty" woman.

Here's another example. In the name of streamlining the NSC, John Bolton, Trump's former security adviser, eliminated the Directorate for Global Health Security and Biodefense, the team responsible for coordinating pandemic preparedness for previous Administrations.

When asked about this move, which has been criticized in the context of his coronavirus response, Trump called the question "nasty." He said, "I don't know anything about it."[41] It was a perfectly legitimate question by the reporter. But it makes Trump look bad, so it becomes to him a "nasty" question. The question isn't nasty, but what it really means is it made Trump feel bad. It's about Trump, not the question. With Trump, his opinions are usually not accurate about the thing itself: they're just barometers of how it makes him feel. The validity of the thing itself is irrelevant to him. Just like the validity of another person is irrelevant to a person with NPD: only the effect on them is relevant.

This is the interpersonal stance of the NPD person. I know what it's like to be under the Administration of a narcissistic entity. I grew up that way. If you're lucky, your needs will coincide with the needs of the person in authority and you'll benefit. If you're unlucky, your needs will be at odds with the leaders, and you'll suffer. But if you expect your leader, who has NPD, to think about and advocate for your needs, when they're different to theirs – well, then you're just out of luck.

With my mother, I decided to separate myself from her, and we no longer talk. It's the best solution for me. Many people have parents that can cause them misery and angst at times. But most of them (certainly not all) have parents that also give them a lot of good stuff as well as the bad stuff. As a result, it can be confusing in deciding how to proceed. If you break those bonds you'll lose a lot as well as gain. It can be a difficult decision, and navigating a way through all this can be tricky. It can be heartbreaking, and involve hard choices and risks.

Not so if you have a parent with NPD, because you aren't getting much in the first place. So breaking away is easier under these circumstances.

---

41 - Mathis-Lilley, Ben. "'I Don't Know Anything About It,' Trump Says About White House's Elimination of Pandemic Response Team," Slate Magazine, March 13, 2020. https://slate.com/news-and-politics/2020/03/i-dont-know-anything-about-it-trump-says-about-his-white-house-eliminating-the-pandemic-response-team.html

Of course it's no picnic, and nobody wants to be in that situation. But the path forward can be clear when you have an NPD parent.

And so it was much the same with me in my move to Canada. When this guy was elected, I knew I had to take action. I knew what kind of person we had chosen to lead us. So my coping mechanism was to separate, as it was with my mother. I chose to remove myself from being under the Administration of a person that wasn't capable of looking out for my interests. I was going to increase my autonomy by becoming more independent. I was going to leave.

Of course, I'm no longer a child and Trump isn't my parent. And Trump isn't a duplicate of my mother. For example, on the positive side, he seems to give more to his children than my mother did, at least in some ways. On the negative side, he's more vindictive, more interested and motivated in revenge against his enemies, than my mother ever was. I also think Trump is crueller.

Another key difference is Trump never had the kind of control over me that a parent has over a young child. But a president can still make decisions, life or death decisions, and certainly quality of life decisions, that will affect the people he leads (for example, see my later chapter on Trump and his management of the coronavirus). And so the parallel, while not exact, is close enough. It is, as the rabbi would say, bad enough.

7

More Canada Stories

Oh Canada! - Immigration, From Both Sides

One of the most gratifying parts of my work in Canada has been conducting psychological assessments for people who are fleeing to Canada from other countries to seek asylum, and safety. I became connected with a Turkish lawyer who works with individuals and families who've been persecuted in Turkey under their increasingly authoritarian leader, Recep Tayyip Erdogan. Erdogan has increasingly cracked down on freedom of speech and anyone criticizing his government, and has persecuted religious minorities and other minorities in his country. Many people in Turkey spoke out for their rights and/or criticized the government. As a result, many of them were jailed, beaten or otherwise abused by Erdogan's police and thugs. As a result of the abuse, many of them suffer from Post-Traumatic Stress Disorder. By assessing them and writing reports for the Canadian immigration board, I can help them start their healing process in Canada.

Below are excerpts from a typical report I wrote, with identifying information obscured to protect the client's confidentiality:

In one incident, Mr. X was distributing papers for the political party he supported. He stated the police took him to the police precinct because he was doing this. When he entered the cell in the police station, he saw other people his age who were covered in blood and he became terrified. He stated he was beaten by a number of police officers and he eventually fainted. His clothes were covered in blood and he had difficulty speaking, he reported. He stated that he was held there for four days. When he went to the hospital for his injuries, the doctor refused to say he saw any injuries and did not treat him, very likely because of political reasons.

In July of 2016, Mr. X was taking photographs of a shootout between the police and the army. Religious extremists were reportedly killing soldiers and Mr. X photographed them. Some of these extremists began punching him as a result.

Mr. X has fearful reactions when he sees things that remind him of his trauma in Turkey. For example, when he sees Canadian police, he begins to panic. He said 'If I see a police officer (in Canada) I walk out of their way, because police is police' – meaning that he experiences no distinction between a police officer in Toronto or Turkey; he simply reacts instinctively with fear. Mr. X said he once had to go to the Ossington police station and he saw the jail cells, and that 'brought back all the memories.' After stating this to me, Mr. X then buried his face in his hands in turmoil.

As is common with many trauma survivors, Mr. X is experiencing other symptoms which are consistent with a diagnosis of PTSD. For example, Mr. X sometimes feels the world is a place in which he cannot trust people. He said he often feels like 'they are going to hurt you.'

The beatings and detentions continued for Mr. X, as described in detail in his narrative. In October 2017 Mr. X finally decided to try to leave Turkey and applied for a Canadian visa. He said his lawyer told him to go abroad or he would risk being killed by the police.

Unlike Mr. X, as bad as I think Trump is, I certainly wasn't being beaten in prison for disagreeing with my government. I'm very, very lucky by comparison. But I fled because I didn't like the road my government was heading down. But where could that road lead? I have a friend from Turkey, and she's told me she thinks Trump wants to be like Erdogan. Or Putin. Or any of the other authoritarian leaders he admires so much.

Trump said of Erdogan, "He's a friend of mine, and I'm glad we didn't have a problem because, frankly, he's a hell of a leader, and he's a tough man, he's a strong man."[42]

Trump befriends Erdogan as he smashes the Turkish people's psyches into pieces in his pursuit of power. Part of my job in Canada is to help pick up a few of these pieces. At least I'm doing my part to compensate for this, umm, "hell of a leader," as my president calls him.

By the way, Trump has declared that Canada is a national security threat to the United States, imposing tariffs on imported Canadian steel and aluminum.[43]

So, let us take stock. We don't only have a president who is pals with Erdogan. We now also have a president who cozies up to Russia but tells us that Canada is our enemy. Christ almighty: America is so fucked up right now.

***

I'm sitting with a patient I find particularly sharp. I really enjoy talking with her; we have a good rapport. We've been working together well for some time now. She asks me how my life is going. She knows that I've been struggling to get my Canadian PR. In this session, I mention the work I do with refugees seeking Canadian citizenship.

She pauses and looks down pensively. She looks back at me, and says something like: "You mean the government will put you in a position of authority to help determine who can become a Canadian citizen, but at the same time put you through all this, scrutinizing you for so long, when you try to become one yourself?"

42 - Finnegan, Conor. "Trump to welcome Erdogan as friend despite high tensions in US-Turkish relations, bipartisan condemnation of Turkey," ABC News, November 13, 2019. https://abcnews.go.com/Politics/trump-erdogan-friend-high-tensions-us-turkish-relations/story?id=66917017
43 - Zakheim, Dov S. "Canada as a national security threat to the United States." The Hill, June 4, 2018. https://thehill.com/opinion/national-security/390527-canada-as-a-national-security-threat-to-the-united-states

I'm quiet, taking this in. Then I reply, "You know, I never thought about that before."

***

I'm sitting on the plane, in the window seat. It's a two seats on each side of the aisle configuration. I always try to sit in the window seat so I can photograph during take off or landing. It's fun for me; photography is my hobby. But during the flight, I'm in my typical half-alive/half-dead airplane trance state. The seat next to me is vacant. It's nice, because I have room. There's one guy in the two seats across the aisle from me. I ignore him. We land.

He says to me, "Excuse me, are you Dr. Stephen Shainbart?" I'm surprised, but I say yes. I don't recognize him. He said, "You were my therapist years ago." He tells me his name. I begin to have a dim recognition. He tells me he has a girlfriend in Toronto. We chat a bit about how the architecture in Toronto is so banal. He talks about how the downtown is turning into a bunch of boring glass condos with no character. I agree heartily. He says, "I think they're going to regret it." I nod.

Later that evening, I thought about it some more. I don't think most Torontonians are going to regret it. For one thing, I don't think most people care about architecture. They should, but they don't. Secondly, I've heard only a few Torontonians even mention how boring their architecture is. I agree with my ex-patient, that it's sad. Even my 15-year-old son, while looking at Toronto's skyline, said, "New York has much more interesting buildings." Of course, those banal condos are all over New York as well. But New York was built up long before Toronto was, and therefore it still has many older buildings.

In Toronto, my son and I, and my ex-client, may be in the minority. I think most Torontonians believe they're living the good life in their downtown glass box condos. Maybe they're better off than us in this regard, because they're happy with it, while we're not. And perhaps this is an example of that relativity I mentioned earlier in the book. If one isn't aware of older, grander architecture, glass box condos don't seem so bad, because there's little else to compare them with. You don't know what you're missing, so you're happy.

Of course, not all Canadians, and Torontonians, are liberal. Or even reasonable. I recently read an article that 86 percent of Canadians disapprove of Donald Trump. I love that. However, what people tend not to realize with numbers like this is that it means that 14 percent of Canadians actually approve of Donald J. ("J" for 'genius') Trump.

I've had a fair number of experiences that go against the liberal Canadian stereotype. For example, I'm in an Uber and I tell the driver I'm an American. He says, "I like your president." I feel this pit in my stomach and a flash of anger. I hide it, and just say, "Oh, tell me why." I start to have a new feeling – curiosity. He tells me how Trump is asserting America's needs in the world, unlike Obama, who just caved in to every other country. He tells me how it's good that he's not letting Canada push the USA around in trade and how he's renegotiating the NAFTA treaty. Finally, he talks about how Trump has brought peace with North Korea. This was around the time Trump was meeting with his newfound friend, Kim Jong-un, and Trump was bragging about how they have a special relationship or whatever. I'd been following the news closely. I had strong doubts that Trump would change anything in the Korean situation, since it had been that way for many decades and Clinton and Bush had both failed miserably. I thought it was more likely, because of his delusions of grandeur, that Trump was fooling himself he was personally going to make peace with North Korea. I worried he'd make a mistake that would hurt the US. But I also thought, "Hey, anything is possible; I can always be wrong. Maybe he'll bring peace. I don't see how, but I can't rule it out as a possibility. I mean, it's within the laws of physics."

Anyway, the driver said, "Yes, they already reached an agreement. There's going to be peace between the US and North Korea. They made the agreement."

I said, "I don't think they actually completed any agreements." "Yes, they did," he said. It's over a year later and the situation in Korea remains exactly the same and many people now think Kim Jong-un simply outplayed Trump. But these experiences demonstrate to me that any Canadian can, of course, be just as stupid and delusional as any American. I just hope there's a smaller percentage of them than in the USA.

I also had a female Uber driver who immigrated to Canada from the Philippines. She told me how she hated Justin Trudeau because he allowed all these refugees into Canada, like the Syrian refugees. She went on about how these immigrants didn't deserve to be there and how they just take Canadian taxpayer dollars and don't work.

"But aren't you an immigrant?" I ask. She said, "Yes. But they should only allow a few immigrants into the country." As a child of an immigrant refugee to the USA, I'm always amazed at the hypocrisy of immigrants who are against immigration.

Finally, I want to point out that even in Toronto, which like NYC is generally to the left of its country, there are a surprising number of people who say some form of the following:

"Trudeau is as bad as Trump." I've encountered this frequently in texting with women on dating sites. It's good to find out, because then I know it's time to swipe left. But I also hear it from regular people when I interact with Torontonians. Not the majority, but I'd say perhaps 20 percent of them.

To me, this shows either that some Canadians have very poor judgment, or at least no perspective on things. Or bad values. Having lived here, I no longer idealize Trudeau. I've learned that he often acts like a typical weaselly politician. For example, he goes forward on fighting climate change while at the same time approving big oil pipelines to appeal to voters. But overall he's still a liberal and sane person. But saying he's as bad as Trump is like comparing the few drops of water that fall on your head while walking on the street from someone's air conditioner above to a monsoon in India.

All of these experiences demonstrate that Canada isn't the monolithic liberal entity that American blue-staters dream about. Of course, intellectually I knew that tribal (and foolish) people are everywhere. But it's another thing to be there and experience it directly in front of your face. Like pimples and blackheads, dickheads can pop up anywhere.

**

I'm at the airport in NYC, going through security. TSA is yelling at everyone, like zookeepers dealing with animals. "Laptops out!" Mine's out already, as I know the drill. The next week I'm at the airport in NYC and I take out my laptop. The TSA, capricious as ever, yells at me, "Don't take the laptop out!" like I'm a moron. You can't win with the TSA. I was hoping that by flying so frequently, I'd learn all the procedures like the back of my hand, to do them efficiently. That way I hoped I'd be yelled at less often. But it's not possible. The rules seem to change randomly, and so the only thing that remains constant is the discomfort of being scolded.

After enduring this inconsistency, of the TSA yelling at me because I take my laptop out, and also being yelled at because I don't take my laptop out, I finally worked up the nerve to inquire about this torture. This particular TSA agent was one of the pleasant ones (there are some). She told me I had to take my laptop out even though I was "pre-check" because often (which is the majority of times) the TSA pre-check line is closed. That's when they give you that green paper so you don't have to take off your shoes. But you still have to take your laptop out. But if you happen to come at one of those off times when pre-check is working, then you don't have to take out your laptop. However, of course, none of these changes are explained in any way that travelers could possibly understand. It would be nice if they did inform the public, but at least now I know the procedure has some rationale for its inconsistency. Of course, as a passenger flying at random times, it makes no difference; it's all arbitrary and we're all going to get yelled at regardless.

Back in Manhattan

My then 13-year-old son Jordan is visiting me in my office building in Manhattan. I tell the security guard in the lobby he'll be coming later that day and described what he looked like, so he could expect him and let him come up to me. Later, my son arrives at my office. After about 20 minutes we go back down to the lobby to travel home, and both of us walk past the security guard.

Me (to Security Guard, "SG"): "So, did he give you any trouble when he came in?"

SG: "Yeah, he started giving me some crap and started with this attitude. But don't worry, I handled it."

Me: "I'm sorry about that. It's not his fault that he's like that. He's messed up in the head. He's kind of a little bit slow. He's got ... problems."

SG: "I noticed. But I didn't want to say anything."

My son laughs. We leave the building, emerging onto 26th Street.

Jordan to me: "See, in Toronto the guard would not joke like that. He would have just said 'Oh, no, he gave me no trouble at all.'"

Me (sadly): "Yeah."

On Canadian Arrogance

Americans tend to think of Canadians as a polite, unassuming people. I think this belief has a basis in reality. My experience is that, on the whole, Canadians are in fact more polite than Americans. They say "Thank you" and, of course, true to the stereotype, they tend to say "sorry" much more than Americans, although it does sound like "saw-ree." Americans do say sorry when they are sorry. Canadians can also say sorry when they mean sorry, but they more often say sorry for many other purposes. Sorry can mean, "You're annoying me," or it can just be a polite way of easing potential social tension, as in pre-empting a conflict.

I guess an example would be two people in each other's way: both people would say "sorry," although both might be actually thinking, "I wish you would get the hell out of my way." But saying sorry kind of pre-emptively diffuses any potential conflict. A New Yorker, by contrast, would be more prone to say, "Hey, watch where you're going."

But there's one group that Canadians don't feel compelled to be polite or respectful of: Americans.

I'm not saying all Canadians are like this, not by a long shot. I would say I've met some, a minority, who talk about actually liking the United States, and probably the biggest group is apathetic. But there's a large anti-Americanism segment here. And, of course, the anti-Americanism is much worse since Trump was elected.

I have read that this anti-Americanism might be based on envy of the United States. The US is ten times bigger in population and in economic output. Justin Trudeau's father, when he was prime minister, compared Canada to a rider on an elephant; you tend to be driven by the elephant. Another explanation I've read is it's an attempt at Canadian identity. There's a lot of writing about the lack of a clear Canadian identity. There are some things that are uniquely Canadian but, compared with other countries, these are relatively few and far between, in my opinion. So much of what's Canadian – the stores, the television shows, the movies, the culture – are heavily Americanized. So perhaps highlighting differences with the United States is one of the ways Canadians can define their own, separate identity.

So, as an American, what have I experienced in Canada? Well, I have one patient that hits me with anti-American remarks virtually every session. Part of this is his way of teasing me, and part of it is his way of avoiding closeness, I believe. But he could have chosen a thousand ways to do this, and it's telling that he chose anti-Americanism as his vehicle to do so. He frequently remarks on how I like guns, and how I must believe differences should be resolved by shooting. And also that I don't believe in science. A common theme is how I must not know much about the world beyond the United States. It's as if he thinks Americans are all a bunch of rural Texans walking around with cowboy hats and guns voting for Trump. Certainly, the USA has its share of these types, but his lack of recognition of how many Americans are like me – leftist, cosmopolitan urbanites – is considerable. He does have some awareness that there are liberal pockets in the USA, but overall he regards the USA as a Republican caricature. I suspect it's not me who's the ignorant one. Especially when one considers that Hillary Clinton won the popular vote by three million people.

(By the way, out of curiosity I looked it up. The population of New York State – which in this case includes the rural, more politically conservative area of upstate New York and liberal New York City – has a higher percentage of passport holders than Canadians. Do you know where the United Nations is located, Canadians? It isn't in Toronto.)

I was at a street fair in Kensington Market, one of my favorite neighborhoods in Toronto. A street performer was doing magic tricks. He told the crowd that he wanted them each to count to three in their native language. So he said, "In other words, if you are Spanish, you say 'Uno, dos, tres.' If you are from Ontario, you would say 'one, two, three.' If you are from the US, you would say 'one, and another one, and another one after that.'" That one was funny, I'll give him that.

I have a Torontonian friend who said she wanted to buy a NASA shirt for her son, but she didn't because she was annoyed that it had an American flag on it next to the NASA symbol. She spoke disdainfully about how Americans need to put their flag on everything. In my view, NASA is an American institution, and it's appropriate to be proud that we are (and remain over 50 years later) the only country that put people on the moon.

You know, when Canada achieves a major breakthrough on that scale, one that no other country is able to achieve, I wouldn't hold it against them if they showed pride in their accomplishment. Maybe part of the reason there is so much American symbolization is that the USA has accomplished so much more than Canada. It may not be simply due to American arrogance, but it may also be due to an imbalance in achievement. Let's see ... that light bulb you Canadians use, what country invented it? That google search you just did, what country created this vast technology? That movie or television show you just watched? No, Canadians, while you can be so smug, you certainly seem quite reliant with the products and inventions created by your neighbor to your south. I wonder if you stop to pause to think what country brought these things into the world, and what country didn't.

One Canadian sent me a humorous clip from *The Daily Show* that had a segment on Americans begging Canada to invade so they could be free. But as I watched it I thought, even *The Daily Show* is an American show that Canadians watch and use to convey their anti-American sentiment.

***

This one stayed with me.

Question:

What's the difference between a bowl of yogurt and a Canadian?

Answer:

At least a bowl of yogurt has its own culture.

***

Here's another way to illustrate the point. If the United States suddenly disappeared from the earth, Canada would almost definitely disintegrate. Its economy is dependent on its trade with the United States. Its national defense is reliant on the United States for protection. If the United States disappeared suddenly, I think Canada would become a Russian colony in less than a week.

But if Canada disappeared suddenly, the United States would be affected, but it would more or less continue on as before. I mean, even the one US state of California is bigger both in population and in economic output than the entire nation of Canada. So again, if you're a smug Canadian feeling superior to the United States, you might want to consider some painful realities.

One person was ranting to me about how polls show how four out of five Canadians want the border with the United States to remain closed because of the coronavirus. In response, I asked him if this was the first time that all five of them were in the same room at once.

I said earlier there's an imbalance in achievement between the two countries, but I want to clarify that. Statistics show that Canadians are, on the whole, happier than Americans and they live longer. That's pretty damned important. I'm reminded of the *Star Trek* saying, "Live long and prosper." Well, overall, Canadians do live longer and prosper more than Americans. On the other hand, Canada lacks a certain glory. So I guess it all depends on your definition of achievement.

I don't think I'd need to, or want to, take the Canadians down a notch, as I'm doing now, if so many of them weren't so smug about how they are better than America. After all, I really like Canada. But after two years of many Canadians feeling quite free to insult my country, even to my face, I've lost my patience. I mean, you guys are supposed to be the nice ones. But it seems to me it's people from the supposedly "nice" country that have this tendency to say mean things about Americans. Americans, on the other hand, who are supposedly the rougher, more arrogant ones, well, if they have any opinion of Canadians at all, it's usually a positive one. We like to talk about how nice Canadians are. I find this whole phenomenon to be ironic.

Another point. There's a prevalent sensibility that I hear from Canadians – that they're also better because they're less boastful than Americans. This irony seems utterly lost on many Canadians. You can't be modest by going around boasting how unboastful you are. You can't be truly humble by talking about how much more worldly, civilized, and informed you are than another group. But it does make you a hypocrite.

I'd say in response, concerning Canada, that never has a country been so prideful and boastful after achieving so relatively little. It's a good country, with many noble features. But when the history of human civilization is written, Canada will not be its first chapter. That's okay, but that reality contrasted with the boastful arrogance of many Canadians is something I find distasteful. I believe the word for this is braggadocio. It's a trait that doesn't suit Canadians well.

I'm not saying all Canadians are like this, not by a long shot. I would say I've met some, a minority, of Canadians who talk about actually liking the United States, and probably the biggest group is apathetic.

But there's a large and vocal anti-Americanism segment here.

As Will Ferguson and Ian Ferguson put it in their humorous book, *How to Be a Canadian*: "You see, in the hypersensitivity of today's all-inclusive Canada, American culture is just about the only thing left that Canadians are allowed to mock. Other cultures are off-limits, but the Americans are still fair game. You can televise one-hour specials with title like *Boy, Americans Sure Are Stupid!* and you will be applauded for your efforts. You can condemn Americans outright and never be accused of being a bigot. So carp away!"[44]

Canada is not Heaven, and Canadians are not Angels, but Canada is Safer than the United States

Most liberal New Yorkers, myself included, thought of Canada as a more liberal and enlightened version of the United States. We thought, if we could set up our own country to be like the liberal blue states, it would resemble Canada.

In what I'm about to say, I want to point out that I'm not attacking Canada. I mean, I sacrificed everything to move there, and actions speak louder than words. I am, however, describing how the picture gets more nuanced as Canada goes from being a blue-stater's fantasy to an actual place with flaws like anywhere else.

I no longer idealize Canada; I have learned it's quite imperfect. I've experienced some flaws first-hand that surprised me. For example, as a psychologist I'm used to sometimes referring my clients to psychiatrists for medication (antidepressants, anti-anxiety meds, etc). In Canada, it was really something for me to hear that it was virtually impossible for anyone to get to see a psychiatrist within six months. Canadians who need to see a psychiatrist are often in a terrible dilemma. They can go see their primary doctor, who sometimes know relatively little about psychiatric medication, or they can wait and suffer for six months. Americans, by contrast, can see

---

44 - Will Ferguson and Ian Ferguson, How to Be a Canadian (Vancouver: Douglas & McIntyre, 2007), 193.

a psychiatrist pretty much immediately (assuming you have health insurance, of course).

Canada has other flaws. I was amazed to learn that in parts of Canada the government operates Catholic schools – religious schools, for educating children. Whatever happened to separation of Church and State? Liberal Americans, starting with Thomas Jefferson, fought for that. It's not really as embedded in Canada. To me, if not for evangelical Republicans, that's a problem.

Canada has its share of racism and intolerance. It's not heaven on earth. Canada totally dicked over their indigenous population. They ripped apart indigenous families and sent their kids away from their families to boarding schools. The indigenous people of Canada suffer much worse from poverty and substance abuse than other Canadians, and like many minority groups in America, they are victims of prejudice. However, unlike Blacks in America, they only constitute five percent of the population. America managed to dick over just about all its minorities.

I do get the strong sense that, overall, Canada is more tolerant and open to immigrants than the United States. It's also less militaristic and warlike than the US. So, in general, I feel I did move to a more tolerant society. Although partisanship in Canada is on the rise, it's still nothing like the extreme partisanship seen in the United States. Overall, but not by as much as I had thought, Canada does seem to be a less extreme, more tolerant, more cohesive, and gentler society than the USA.

But I don't think that Canadians are naturally born to be better people than Americans. If this is the case, it brings up an important question. Why did Canadians turn out to be more tolerant and less militaristic than Americans? In my view, part of the answer to this is that Canadians got lucky in some ways. I've been shocked to see how few Canadians are aware of the good fortune that may be behind their gentler nature. Instead, many just assume they're "better" than America. I think that's pretty simplistic, and the truth is full of reasons that make it more complicated.

For one thing, slavery never took root here like it did in the United States. But this is not because Canadians are better people. It's just that, like the northern United States, the colder climate made economic conditions unfavorable toward slavery. So Canada is more like blue-state America this way. Canada also has a much smaller Black population than the United States as a result. All of this probably contributes to less racial tension.

But here's another huge factor to consider. Mexico lies on the southern border of the United States. Mexico is a relatively poor country, with millions of refugees, both legal and illegal, seeking to enter the country to its north, the United States, to seek a much better life.

By contrast, what country lies on the southern border of Canada? The United States does, not Mexico. This makes a big difference. Canada doesn't have nearly the problem the United States has involving a huge influx of people desperately trying to flood their country. To Canada's north is the North Pole, and only Santa Claus lives there – and he's a sweetheart. On the east and west lie vast oceans. Canada is protected, safe, and is largely left alone.

As a result of all this, Canada can easily regulate who comes into the country and doesn't have to feel threatened by outsiders. Canadians, relative to Americans, can more easily control their situation. When one is in a privileged situation, one can afford to be more generous and open-minded.

I'm not defending the vicious hatred that Trump and his people have brought upon us regarding treatment of Mexicans and other ethnic groups. Not in a million years. What I'm saying is that it's much easier for Canadians to be more tolerant than Americans because they're under far less pressure.

Canadians also like to compare themselves favorably to the United States as being a more peace-loving country. Fair enough. But like immigration policy, there are reasons behind their different attitude other than they were just born as nicer people than Americans. Think about this: I think it's a lot easier to be less militaristic and more peaceful when the most powerful country in the world is right next to you and is committed to your defense. If anyone invaded Canada, the United States would be there in a second to defend it, if only for its own interests if not Canada's. As a result, no one is going to invade Canada. It's illuminating to note that Australia, which has a smaller population than Canada, has a larger military, because it's an island country on the other side of the world.

A dramatic illustration of all this involves Canada's navy. Canada has by far the biggest coastline of any country in the world, with more than 202,000 km. By comparison, Indonesia is a distant second, with about 54,000 km of coastline. Despite this, Canada's navy is surprisingly weak.[45] It's naval forces are as small as its coastline is big. According to the *National Post*, a Canadian newspaper, Canada's navy is divided into two parts, the Pacific and the Atlantic navies. The tiny country of Singapore "easily trounces" Canada's Canadian Pacific fleet, with more and faster ships. As far as Canada's eastern navy, Azerbaijan, which is a landlocked country with no ocean access, equals Canada's 15 warships.

As I mentioned previously, Australia, with a significantly smaller population and GDP than Canada, has a more powerful military, and this includes their navy. The article's explanation for this matches what I previously mentioned.

So what could explain this enormous disparity between Canada's huge coastline and its tiny fleet? To quote the article: "Most importantly, the Aussies fluff up their naval budget with the full knowledge that, if something goes down, they can't simply wait for the Americans to save them."

As a result of their reliance on American military protection, Canada is able to redirect its dollars to things like national healthcare and its heavily subsidized universities, among other things, instead of more fully contributing to its own defense. I wonder how many Canadians, especially those who are most vociferous in their smug anti-Americanism, consider all of this.

---

45 - https://nationalpost.com/news/canada/
at-least-we-could-invade-new-zealand-how-small-is-the-royal-canadian-navy-really

To be fair, I also think there's something less warlike in the Canadian character than in the American character. Some people may see this as a blessing, and some as a curse. I think it cuts both ways. The United States was born from violent revolution, while the history of Canada is more effective than Ambien for putting one to sleep. A lot of people died to enable Americans to seize their freedom a century before Britain granted freedom to Canada. In my view, deciding which one is better is complicated. But there may be something less assertive in the Canadian character, yielding a more accepting, less belligerent attitude.

My overall point is that Canada isn't necessarily better than the United States, like many liberal New Yorkers tend to think. Nor is it worse. It's just a bit different. But due to a mixture of lucky circumstances like the ones I mentioned above, it may be a relatively safer and saner place to live in than the United States, at least for now. And especially under Trump. And that's why I went there.

***

I'm sitting next to a fairly attractive woman, mid-thirties. She's reading the book "Sapiens" by Yuval Noah Harari. I was thinking about reading this book. For her to be reading this book, I figure she's probably a bright and intellectually curious person. We start talking. I'm not a shy guy, but I'm not extraverted either. Being trapped on a plane next to someone I don't find interesting is unpleasant, even a bit painful for me. As a result, I usually don't initiate conversation, because I don't find it worth the risk. But she seemed smart, and I was truly interested in the book. So I asked her about the book.

We're having a good conversation, about the book, ideas, and also life in Toronto. I feel good talking with her. The flirty feeling is there but minimal for me, and after 15 minutes she mentions her boyfriend. I experience a momentary feeling of disappointment but then a stronger feeling of relief – now I no longer have to worry about coming across as attractive and desirable. More importantly, maybe I can make a friend in my new city. I'm a bit nervous, but as we're landing, I tell her I really enjoyed talking to her and find her bright and interesting. I tell her I know she has a boyfriend so I ask her not to misunderstand; I'm not interested in her that way. I ask if she'd be interested in exchanging phone numbers and see about being friends.

"I don't think so," she replies. I look at her, a bit stunned. Then I think about all the work I did in therapy, and I tell myself this doesn't matter. But my feelings are ahead of my thoughts, and I'm a little bit hurt. I just want to get away. She walks ahead of me out of the plane. She stops, and says, "I hope that's okay." I nod and keep walking out of the gate.

I thought to myself, I may be a confident New Yorker and all that, but building a new and happy life in a new city, a new country, is not going to be easy.

On Canadian Kindness (it's real)

A) I'm at Billy Bishop Airport (the small one). I'm early so I decide to get a bagel with cream cheese and what they call "smoked salmon", which is properly known as a "bagel with lox" in New York City. There's a line and I wait my turn for the cashier. I have my typical gear with me: my carry-on suitcase and my backpack. When I finally get to the cashier, I hand her cash and she says "no cash, only cards." I make a slightly frustrated face and move to the side and start to put down my stuff to get my wallet. The woman behind me advances to the cashier and says to me, "Don't worry about it, I got it." And then she paid for me.

It all happened so fast. After a moment I recovered and I said "Are you kidding?" And she said "no." And I said, "Wait, can I ask you a question?" And she said sure. And I said, "Are you Canadian?" And she smiled and said "yes." And I replied, "Now it makes sense," and I smiled at her. I then said, "I would argue with you about repaying you but this is going to make a good story when I get back to New York." And then I said, "Thank you" and walked away. I got back to NYC and put it on my Facebook, and people said it was indeed a good story.

B) I'm a pescatarian, but boy do I miss cheeseburgers. Down the block from my apartment in Toronto is an A&W chain (apparently, in

Canada, A&W is a fast food chain. In NYC, A&W is a soda – "pop" in Canada – company). It's open 24/7 and sells Beyond Meat Burgers, which I love, love, love. It's 2 a.m. and I go for a Beyond Meat Burger run. There's nobody there except me, the food workers, and the security guard. I give the cashier my American Debit Visa card and it's declined. My card usually works in Canada, but it's just rejected by their system. I have no Canadian cash, just American cash. I ask if they will take American cash (most places in Toronto do, although they'll rip you off with the exchange rate). They say no. I'm frustrated. I think for a minute, and I say "I'll go to the ATM; I'll be back in a few minutes."

The security guy says to me: "Hold it!" I freeze. I've learned from the airports to obey these uniformed, authority types. I stop and say, "Yes?" He then puts up his hand, silently indicating for me to wait. I'm not sure what's going on, but I tell myself I'll find out. He places his order with the woman behind the counter.

He finishes. He then turns to me and says, "I just ordered and bought your food along with my dinner." I say, "Really?" I'm not quite as shocked as I was at Billy Bishop airport (this having happened before). I'm transitioning from confusion to delight. I say, "Thank you, that's very kind of you." He says, "Canadian hospitality." Indeed. Canadian hospitality is genuinely lovely and a joy to experience, especially for a jaded New Yorker.

Money and Love

I expected the entire process of moving to Canada to take between a year and a year and a half. It ended up taking more than two years. And this is important – if there ever was a case of "time is money," this was it. Every week I wasn't a Canadian permanent resident meant I couldn't start to earn better money. This is because you cannot own a business, including private practice, unless you're a Canadian permanent resident or citizen. What this boiled down to was for as long as I was still not a PR, I had to fly to NYC, see my private patients, make money, stay in an Airbnb or hotel, and fly back. This amounted to an enormous amount of time and money over two years.

For more than two years I didn't get to live in any one city for more than three or four days at a time.

This situation played out on a number of fronts and ended up shaping my life in ways I'd never experienced before. Ways that I wouldn't wish on my worst enemy.

First of all, this entire project financially devastated me. I've never been great with saving money. And most of my potentially disposable income went to child support for my son. So, by the time I got my permanent residency, I'd spent whatever savings I had when this process began. Depleted isn't the right word. Gone is more like it.

I started dating a woman around this time. As things progressed, I felt I had to tell her about my financial situation. I told her it was hard for me to tell her about it because I was embarrassed and felt badly about myself in this one area. I also was anxious because I felt she may judge me negatively or even reject me.

You know what she said? "Really? You mean I'm supposed to look down at you and be more attracted to somebody who doesn't like his job or his life and just works for the man and saves money over time? Instead of somebody who goes after his dream and makes it happen?"

This helped me a lot. It was the opposite message, the antidote to the message I was raised with by my mother. I knew it already, but in my moment of self-doubt, it was exactly what I needed to hear. She's a lovely woman, but we've since broken up. However, I'll always be grateful for her words.

The Airbnb

In terms of financial pressure, the first year was not so bad. I still had some savings. But, over the year, I spent it down. As I said before, I was under the impression the whole process would take a year; a year and a half, tops. So I budgeted (more or less) for that time frame. I'd take taxis to and from the airports – sometimes. When traveling so often, reducing the amount of time getting to and from the airport helped make things more bearable. Especially in NYC, where the infrastructure is medieval and getting to and from LaGuardia can take 90 minutes by mass transportation. I stayed in my apartment in Brooklyn, but I'd stay in Airbnbs in Toronto. That way, at least I still had my home, my comfort, at least some of the time.

However, during the second year, which I'd not expected to go through, all of that evaporated. I realized I'd not be able to survive financially unless I started renting out my Brooklyn apartment. I met with my landlord (ghettolord is more like it) to ask his permission to Airbnb it. That went well. His approach as a landlord was that he didn't care at all about anything – not fixing things in the apartment, not renovating anything – as long as he got his money. So I was fortunate he was consistent – he didn't care at all if I Airbnb'd my place as long as he got his money. Finally, I saw the advantage in having a ghettolord.

My first Airbnb guests were this pleasant young Latino couple on their first visit to NYC. I spent a lot of time buying things for the place: fancy soap dishes, toothbrush holders, towels, linens, etc. I paid for a good cleaning lady. I wrote to them a well-thought-out list of things to do in NYC, using my native knowledge. I greeted them and showed them around. Then I flew to Toronto.

A few days later, I got a text and phone call from them. My neighbor, who has a history of psychiatric hospitalizations, called the NYC police on them, saying there were intruders in my apartment. My Airbnb guests told me the NYPD came and interrogated them harshly. When they offered to prove to them on their phone that they were legitimate Airbnb guests, the cops remained harsh and suspicious and threatened to arrest them. They were terrified. I had to attest over the phone that they were not intruders.

They demanded their money back – almost $1,000. They threatened to write up a report on the Airbnb site for future potential guests about what they just went through if I didn't refund them. I gave them their money back.

I wrote my neighbor a note and asked him not to do this again, and told him that future guests would be coming. I wasn't sure if that would actually make a difference, given his difficulties, but fortunately it did.

Nevertheless, it's fair to say this was not an auspicious beginning to my Airbnb career.

Airbnb (and my shoes) are inkblot tests

As a psychologist, I was trained in administering the Rorschach inkblot test. You know, the one in which the psychologist asks the person, "What do you see in this inkblot?" The idea is that the inkblot is an ambiguous entity that the patient projects their psychological issues onto, and they see what they want to see in it. This is supposed to reveal how their mind works.

In psychology graduate school, I expected to learn about how people see things differently by studying their responses to the Rorschach test. I didn't expect, however, to learn even more about people by Airbnbing my apartment.

I lived in my Brooklyn apartment for nearly ten years. When I came back home to Brooklyn from Toronto, I had my stuff there. I left my clothes in the closets, my books on the bookshelves, and so on. I had no intention of clearing everything out to make it look like a hotel. I needed to maintain a sense of home to keep my sanity. But I said as much on the Airbnb listing. I made it clear that this Airbnb rental was also my home.

The apartment itself, like the inkblot, was the same for everyone. How people saw it, however, was certainly not the same. Welcome to Projection City.

Here are some actual quotes (I changed or abbreviated the names to protect privacy):

Sarah:

> *"The apartment was clean and cute in really delightfully odd ways (if you love an older house with fun corners and niches and angles, you're going to have a blast exploring this place!) and the neighborhood was*

absolutely perfect for everything we wanted to do. The living room couch is extraordinarily comfy; I actually chose to sleep there rather than the bed one night, it was like a cloud! The host was very helpful and got right back to us very quickly when we had a little trouble with the internet. Thank you again for a great stay!"

Same apartment, reviewed by **Lucy**:

"DO NOT RENT THIS APARTMENT!! We arrived at the apartment at 11pm after taking a taxi, the neighborhood was quite cloudy, it was scary to walk around, I thought someone would appear to rob us at any moment ... The apartment when entering was super messy, when entering on the right there was a kind of furniture carrying things thrown there, books, magazines, coins, figures of everything, it seemed that someone had been there for a moment and had everything messy. The TV cabinet was full of dust, the sofa looked like a herd of elephants had passed over it and was made of suede or corduroy, I don't remember, and it was super dirty. We went upstairs to the room, the stairs squeaked a lot that looked like they were going to break, and the light in the room didn't work. The terrace I looked for but I did not see it, it must be of the nerves but I doubt that it was clean and as well as in the photo the truth. There was also a bug that I don't know what it was but it looked like a scorpion. I told the owner all this, and all he said was that I was threatening him ... Thanks to him I had to pay a money in a hotel to be able to be 10 days. If you do not want to waste money .... I do not recommend going to anyone and if it is with children much less. The arrival of the trip ruined me."

I think my favorite discrepancy between them is:

"The living room couch is extraordinarily comfy; I actually chose to sleep there rather than the bed one night, it was like a cloud!"

Vs.

"The sofa looked like a herd of elephants had passed over it and was made of suede or corduroy, I don't remember, and it was super dirty."

Although her seeing a scorpion, an animal which lives in the desert, in my Brooklyn apartment might be an even better projection. I have to wonder what she'd see in the inkblots.

One visitor, from Holland, threatened to report me to Airbnb and write a bad review unless I gave him a full refund. He complained of it being filthy. When I asked him why he thought this, and demanded a full refund, he replied that some of the light switches were dirty with handprints on them. He sent me a photo of a light switch with grease on it. And the request for a full refund.

Moving on, **Dave from Ireland** wrote:

> *"My partner and I spent ten wonderful days at Stephen's apartment in Brooklyn. From the moment we stepped inside we felt at home. The spacious, inviting downstairs area was warm and welcoming. We were able to feel quite at home there and it was so convenient to local transportation, that our visit was made so much better. We spent many hours exploring the neighborhood and felt safe and comfortable doing so. Then in the evening we'd return to the apartment and chill out for the evening, either inside in the air-conditioned downstairs or out the back in the patio area. We would like to thank Stephen most sincerely for letting us stay in his beautiful home and we would strongly recommend this apartment to anyone seeking a comfortable, home from home experience. We will definitely be back again."*

The last straw for me, however, was this review by **Nina**:

> *"Unfortunately this was not a particularly comfortable apartment. The photos convey a cozy space, and there are things about it that are nice, but it is a fairly dingy basement apartment that is cluttered with a lot of books, mementos, and other things that tend to collect in one's home. The patio space, which is a selling point, was unusable! It was overgrown with weeds and littered with dried leaves, dirt and dead plants. This place needs a good clean up of clutter and some attention to detail to welcome visitors. We were booked for three nights and we left a day early. This place is not ready for prime time."*

That's it, I had had it. I had to respond. And I enjoyed writing every sentence. I have italicized my favorite ones.

Response from Stephen:

"I am sorry that you had a disappointing experience in my apartment. I always do my best to provide my guests with a pleasant experience, but sometimes I am not able to do so. This is one of those times. Some of your statements are accurate and some are not. Allow me to address them for the benefit of future potential guests. I want every potential guest to make the best decision for their needs.

"First, you describe the Airbnb as a 'basement apartment.' It is actually a 'garden apartment.' Brownstoner, which is a leading Brooklyn real estate publication, gives a really good definition: 'In Brooklyn, a garden apartment most often means the ground floor of a townhouse with access to the backyard, but it can have a broader meaning as well. In Brooklyn, townhouse garden apartments are typically on the ground floor or slightly below it, and may lack the soaring ceilings of the parlor-level room. A garden duplex, for example, would include all of that plus the parlor floor.' This describes my apartment very well. It is a garden duplex as defined above. It is two steps below the ground level; it is not the basement. In fact, there is a basement below the apartment. The upstairs part of the duplex, where the bedroom is, is on the second floor, and it has high ceilings. This is not a basement by any means. However, to all potential guests, please note the following: *If you are seeking an Airbnb with a backyard, you will in fact have to stay on the ground level and not an upper floor of a building. Here's my reasoning: the ground level is where the ground is located.*

"Moving on to other concerns, you wrote: 'that is cluttered with a lot of books, mementos, and other things that tend to collect in one's home.' This is accurate. I do indeed have books in the bookshelves in my apartment. I also have some personal mementos as well. I fully admit this. As stated in the profile, I live in my apartment when I am not renting it out as an Airbnb. If you require a place that lacks personal belongings, please consider a hotel. *If you are planning on renting someone's personal apartment, please be advised that you may see some of their personal belongings. In fact, I would suggest that any potential guest who becomes agitated or offended by the presence of books on book-shelves avoid my apartment at all costs.*

"Finally, as to the outdoor space. It is true that weeds grow in the backyard while I am away for periods of time. I do prune the weeds as best I can from the main backyard space where people lounge, but some weeds remain on the perimeter of the backyard. It is also true that one might find some dried leaves – or even dirt – in the backyard. Please ask yourself if you feel that this makes it "unusable" to you. And please ask yourself if you will be unhappy to have your own private backyard – in New York City – because there you may find dirt and dried leaves there, for the price I am charging – before you consider my place. However, if you feel you can find some pleasure in such a place, please consider staying in my home. Thank you."

I think it's important to inform people of the fact they may encounter dirt in a backyard. It's kind of like a public service announcement.

Another inkblot moment, but not involving an Airbnb. One of my clients stated that he feels he should never point out when someone is doing something well, because that should always be expected, but if something is done wrong, something should always be said. So he blurts out in the middle of the session: "You need to shine your shoes!"

Pissed me off. The same day, a few hours later, wearing the same shoes, I saw another client. She came in, said hi, and then even before sitting down, said, "I really like your shoes!"

I think that moment cemented for me the idea that I won't give a shit most of the time what anyone else thinks. Life can be one big inkblot. It's crazy out there. After all, Trump was elected by the people to be the fucking president of the United States.

Sadness

My life was very, very hard during the second year. I was almost never able to stay in my Brooklyn apartment. In fact, I had no consistent home of any kind. Because of financial pressures, I had to rent out both my Brooklyn apartment and stay in Airbnbs when I was in Toronto as well. Therefore, I'd typically stay in Airbnbs all the time, throughout my stays in both cities. In New York, I'd typically stay in someone's bedroom, because renting my own apartment or hotel room every single night over a year was just too expensive. So I lived out a suitcase and never had a familiar and comfortable place to exist.

My discomfort was cumulative. As time wore on, I was being worn down. I always felt in a state of dis-ease. And sometimes the people in the rest of the apartment were not easy to be with.

I remember my low point quite well. I was staying in a crappy apartment in outer Brooklyn. There were people in their twenties partying in the living room outside my door. They were loud and high and I was miserable. I went to the bathroom and saw shit stains all over the toilet.

I was 56 years old, and this is what my life had come to. I honestly believe most people would've given up well before this point. I'm not sure how much of my tenacity was due to an extraordinary drive and how much of it's due to a masochistic streak. I'm sure it's a little bit of both. And, as I said, I suffered so much I'm not sure it was all worth it. All I know is that it would have been a lot worse if I went through all this sacrifice and failed. At least I accomplished my goal. I'm proud of myself.

I remembered when I started to contemplate going on this whole journey to become Canadian. I figured I had gotten my PhD in my twenties and thirties, raised a child in my forties, and I had just enough energy left for one last giant life project. I believe this is the last long-term, difficult project of my life. I want to have a more comfortable, more normal life for the rest of my days.

Although you never know what life will bring.

Crossing the Finish Line

One of the last things I had to do to get my Canadian permanent residence was to get the paperwork signed and approved by a Canadian official. I don't understand why they can't just send you a completed document once you're approved. Anyway, you have to get it signed after you receive the papers. One might think that this involves going to a government office and getting it signed. That would make sense, wouldn't it? But, of course, that's not the process.

My lawyer told me the procedure is that one has to leave Canada to become a Canadian permanent resident. She said then I must re-enter the country and get the paperwork signed at a border crossing. Looking back at this now, I wonder why it didn't occur to me to even ask why this was the procedure. Why would you have to leave the country and then return to it? I think I didn't question it because my training was complete. I'd finally reached the point, for better or for worse, where I no longer questioned why the Canadian government does things the way it does them. I only wanted to do whatever it said I should do as quickly as possible.

I told my lawyer I'd rent a car, drive to Buffalo, about an hour-and -a-half drive from Toronto, turn around, re-enter the country, and get the papers signed. She advised me not to do that, however. She said the land crossings to and from the United States had become in recent years like "The Wild West" and that whether the document would be signed depended on the whims of the particular border guard. She said I could try it, but she'd hate to see me possibly drive for three hours for nothing.

I'd been working on this project for three years. I'd been stalled because the system to ensure that psychologists coming into Canada have enough experience actually favors psychologists with almost no experience. I was treated like a criminal at the airport because I was going to eat a plum on the plane. I'd been blocked for months because I have nipples. I trusted nothing in Alice's Wonderland.

It was the afternoon and I was at work at the clinic. I had patients scheduled for the next morning. I went on Momondo, which is probably the best app to book airplane tickets. I booked my flight to NYC for that very evening. I booked my hotel next to LaGuardia airport and slept in NYC. I flew back to Toronto from LaGuardia the next morning.

Just one last, final stupid bureaucratic thing and one final stupid expense (about $500 USD between the airfare and hotel), I told myself.

And so I flew back to Pearson airport. I went to the border guard office with my paperwork. I waited about half an hour. The border guard called me to her desk. I was ready for another unpleasant border guard interaction.

She was lovely. She said she hadn't seen too many Americans becoming Canadian permanent residents. We chatted awhile. She said she was from a distant suburb and didn't like working in Toronto. Toronto was too crowded and urban for her (never mind that, as I mentioned, my Brooklyn-based son said "I love coming up to Toronto. It's so relaxing. It's like going away to the country.") I nodded my assent; of course Toronto was too crowded. Anything to get the paper signed.

We talked more about my flying back and forth to New York. Her face lit up. Suddenly, she had a great idea. She asked me, "Have you tried flying Porter from the island airport? I've never done it myself, but I hear it's wonderful. It will be much easier for you."

I said "Yes, I have. It's wonderful. It's so much easier for me. Thank you!"

I got the damned paper signed. And this is how I became a Canadian permanent resident. Finally.

8

A Plea to Torontonians:
Stop This Barbaric Practice

In my view, Torontonians are a polite and gentle people, especially when compared with New Yorkers. Nevertheless, there are a substantial minority of them that engage in a distasteful, even barbaric practice. I will explain this unfortunate behavior among some Torontonians but, to do so, I must first explain some history for context.

As I said, I'm a life-long New Yorker, born in Manhattan. I've lived in Manhattan, the Bronx, Brooklyn, and the suburb of Long Island. My father and grandfather were both big baseball fans. My grandfather was a New York Giants baseball fan. He'd watch them play in Manhattan. My father, when he came to Brooklyn from Europe at age 18, learned about and then came to love baseball and the Brooklyn Dodgers. Becoming familiar with baseball was part of his assimilation as an immigrant to the United States. Both the Giants and the Dodgers played in the National league.

Sometimes when my father would watch the game on TV, my grandmother would try to talk to him in Yiddish. She'd struggle to get his attention because he was caught up in watching his new sport. She'd get annoyed, having no idea or patience for why he would want to do this instead of listening to her. She'd try to talk to him, and he'd ignore her and continue to watch the game. Finally, with exasperation, she'd say, "Again the game with the stick! Again with the stick!"

Anyway, in the same year – 1958 – both teams abandoned New York. The Brooklyn Dodgers moved to Los Angeles and the New York Giants moved to San Francisco.

Fuck them.

I was born in 1963. But I can remember that time in 1958 as clearly as if it was yesterday, because it lives in the collective unconscious memory of many New Yorkers. I was devastated. Then, after four years in which New York was suffering in a way someone with a phantom limb suffers, the New York Mets were created in 1962 to replace the beloved Dodgers and Giants. The Mets are the offspring of these two teams, and they play in Queens, New York. Indeed, the Mets colors are a hybrid of the colors from these two teams: Dodger Blue and Giants Orange. You see, my lineage, my heritage, is as New York as can be. I love the Mets. My connection to my grandfather and father, and my boyhood memories of going to Mets games with these two men, is full of love for them and for my team. I'm filled with a deep joy to continue this tradition with my son, who's also a huge Mets fan.

As I mentioned, New York does have another baseball team, the New York Yankees, who play in the other league: the American League. You may have heard of the Yankees. I realize I run a risk of alienating a significant base of my audience by saying this, which is why I'm sure I won't be leading with it in marketing this book. I hate the Yankees. Possibly this emotion is similar to the animosity some Canadians have toward the United States. Mets fans, like Canadians, sit in the shadow of an enormous, better-known, and more successful entity.

The difference, I think, is that Americans don't go around targeting Canadians saying, "Ha, ha, we are more successful than you Canadians! You're losers and we're winners!" or messages to that effect. If anything, we say, "You're Canadian? We love you guys. You're all so … nice." However, many Yankees fans go around putting down Mets fans. Moreover, as anyone familiar with the game of baseball knows, the

Yankees have had a huge financial advantage over the Mets, and over most other teams in baseball. Their payroll is much bigger, sometimes twice or three times the size of other teams. With this financial advantage, they can do all kinds of things that other teams can't. For example, they poach the best players that other teams develop in their minor league farm systems, by offering them more money. When one of their players gets injured or underperforms, they can just go out and buy another superstar, while most teams must make do with what they have. Nevertheless, their fans go on bragging.

You know the saying, "It's not whether you win or lose, it's how you play the game." Some Yankees fans, particularly the loudmouths, seem to invert that. "It's whether you win, not how you play the game," would be a sentiment embraced by this type of Yankees fan. Being a winner, not a loser, is all that matters, because their self-esteem is based on this. Other qualities besides winning that some people base their self-esteem upon – like loyalty, devotion, and tenacity to a cause that you believe in, even if you don't succeed – are often strangely absent.

To be fair, certainly not all Yankees fans are arrogant pricks. Some actually grew up rooting for their team before they were financially dominant and, when they didn't win all the time, those fans were fine.

Hey, wait a minute. Hmmm. You know, there's something very familiar here. Let me think … Basing your self-esteem exclusively, almost frantically, on being a "winner" and not a "loser." Ignoring how you play the game, or being unable to see the value of fighting for a cause, whether you succeed or not. Hmmm. This is all really reminding me of someone. Now who could that be? It's certainly not the Mets, that baseball team from Queens. Although it sure does sound like a certain individual, a former real estate developer also from Queens, the more I think about it.

Anyway, I have a comeback for this arrogant subtype of Yankees fan. When they say, "So, you're a Mets fan! You're a loser! So sorry! We have 27 World Series Championship rings! Blah Blah Blah!" I like to reply (I read this on the internet somewhere): "I'm sorry, what's your first and last name again?" And when they say it, I then say, "I am confused. I didn't see your name on the Yankees line-up card. What position did you play for them?" When they stop to consider this, I say, "Because if you didn't play for them, what actually did you do that makes you a winner?" If the timing is right, I'll add, "It seems to me you did the easiest thing in the world: deciding to root for the team that wins, and then take credit for it, as if you somehow actually had anything to do with it."

So, what does any of this have to do with Toronto? Well, it turns out that Toronto has its own baseball team, the Toronto Blue Jays, and they're in the same baseball division as the New York Yankees: the American League East. Therefore, the Yankees are the direct rivals of the Blue Jays. The Mets, by contrast, are in the other League, and therefore have very little to do with the Blue Jays. And of course, the Blue Jays' budget, like most teams, is dwarfed by the Yankees' budget. Unsurprisingly, the Yankees, along with the also wealthy Boston Red Sox, tend to dominate the American League East division, which leaves the Blue Jays unable to win often.

And yet, as I walk around Toronto, I see a fair amount of people wearing Yankees hats, their city's direct rivals. But there they are, this subset of dopehead Torontonians, strolling around wearing them. Do they not know they have their own goddamned team? It would be like having thousands of New Yorkers walking around New York City wearing Philadelphia Phillies caps. It just doesn't happen. But it happens here in Toronto.

I'm guessing that this is largely because the Yankees are a "brand" as well as a team. People wear that Yankees hat in Indonesia, and Uganda, having no idea what the hell it means, except perhaps "New York." But in Indonesia or Uganda, you don't have your own team, from your own city, directly competing against the Yankees. In Toronto you do.

Torontonians, please, please, I implore you to stop this barbaric practice. I'm considering going up to a person in Toronto wearing a Yankees hat and saying, "Oh, you must be from New York; I'm from

New York too!" in an excited voice. When they reply, "No, I'm from Toronto," I'll say, "Oh, do you not like your city? Or do you dislike the Blue Jays in particular? You know the Yankees are the rivals of the Toronto Blue Jays, right?"

I'll do it if necessary. Don't force my hand. Please just stop this unseemly behavior. You Canadians are supposed to be more civilized than this.

Of course, if on the off-chance the person is actually from New York, I'll let it go, right there and then. As a Canadian permanent resident, if I get in trouble and get arrested, I could lose my status. And as I try to remind myself, it's best to not go out of your way to antagonize Yankees fans. Like provoking the mentally ill on the subway, it's usually best to let them rant and just stay out of their way.

Especially in New York's subway.

If Torontonians want to go for a real, authentic New Yorker look, and not just a brand, I advise them to wear a Mets hat instead, emblazoned with the same "NY" symbol that the New York Giants, and now the New York Mets, proudly wear.

I figure that if I can just help even one Torontonian from mindlessly putting on a Yankees hat, then writing this whole book would've been worth it. After all, in the Talmud, a core work of Judaism, there's a saying that to save one life is like saving the whole universe. Same idea here.

9

Coronavirus

When I first conceptualized this book, there was no coronavirus situation. Well, what can I say? Words fail. In many ways, as we all know, the coronavirus situation changed everything. And yet, Donald J. Trump is still the man at the helm during this crisis. The Trump factor is still, as he'd say, "Yuge."

Regarding the coronavirus, I do have some personal things to say. However, I must first point out, in a very un-Trump like way, that whatever I went through is nothing compared with how many others have suffered because of the virus. And my heart goes out to them.

For more than two years, I traveled constantly, back and forth, between New York City and Toronto, as I described previously. For much of that time, I had no consistent home. I'd go from one Airbnb to another, living out of a suitcase or backpack. I was desperate to have a life where I could just stay in one place.

Be careful what you wish for, they say. I most certainly have gone from one extreme to the other in terms of lifestyle. From never having a consistent home for more than a few days at a time to sheltering in place. You never know what life will bring.

I gave up my Brooklyn apartment, after about ten years, at the end of December 2019. In January 2020 I moved to Toronto full-time. I was very excited to start a new and normal life in my new city. I was looking forward to going out and exploring the city, not in a rushed kind of way because I was there for a few days, but as a full-time city resident. The restaurants, the bars, everything. My apartment is downtown, on Yonge Street. Yonge Street is literally in the center of the city; it divides the city into east and west the way Fifth Avenue does in Manhattan.

Well, that didn't happen. By March everything in Toronto was closed down, same as in New York and a million other places. I could've been living anywhere, like everyone else, because we were all pretty much stuck in our homes. It's summer 2020 now and things are very, very slowly beginning to reopen. I don't know when I will get to enjoy Toronto and Canada in the way I'd been planning on.

I have, however, been able to live through the Covid-19 situation as a Canadian and not an American, and for that I'm grateful, with some major exceptions. This is probably the first concrete benefit emanating from my decision to move to a country that's not as dysfunctional as the United States is now.

Seeing how things were handled so differently in Canada only served to bring Trump's actions into even sharper focus. There were so many mistakes and errors in judgment, as well as ridiculous statements and actions by the President to address this virus crisis, that I was dreading writing this section. I struggled with how to choose which stupid things he'd done to write about. And, besides that, I've no doubt there'll be so many poor decisions and tragic consequences which have yet to come, that whatever I write now will be obsolete by the time you read this. But I have to try, at least briefly, to survey them, and to point out how they are "old wine in new bottles" – more of the same Trump pattern.

Trump minimized the coronavirus crisis because he didn't want it to be perceived as a problem that could interfere with his chances of being elected. Again, his needs, as always, come before anyone else's. He also pushed to reopen the economy way too quickly, because a strong economy was a selling point for his re-election campaign. This, of course, only exacerbated the spread of the virus, as we see in the south and west. He refused to wear a mask for months, as a way to demonstrate his "masculinity." Ridiculous and childish. Moreover, by not wearing a mask as President of the United States, he role-modeled for millions of Americans exactly the wrong way to handle the pandemic. These are just a few examples right off the top of my head of the ways he damaged the well-being of the United States and its people. Most informed readers know of these events. But I'd like to emphasize how all of these misjudgments are manifestations of Trump's disturbed psyche.

In other words, the coronavirus was finally an external event, a world event, which brought out the extreme danger of having such a person in charge. I believe Trump and the country were lucky, in that as bad as his decisions were, the coronavirus was the first event which, when combined with Trump's issues, resulted in a full-scale calamity for the American people. And from my vantage point in Canada, which isn't being led by a dysfunctional leader, I feel very sad for my country and for my fellow Americans. Allow me to go into a bit more detail about all of this.

We all know the virus appeared in China months before it emerged in the United States. But the US did virtually nothing to prepare for it.

The Washington Post[46] reported that Trump received more than a dozen warnings about Covid-19 in January and February. Yet he continually downplayed the virus and its dangers.

Remember the things he said?

Jan. 22

"We have it totally under control. It's one person coming in from China, and we have it under control. It's going to be just fine."

Feb. 10

"Looks like by April, you know, in theory, when it gets a little warmer, it miraculously goes away."

March 10

"We're prepared, and we're doing a great job with it. And it will go away. Just stay calm. It will go away."

---

46 - https://www.washingtonpost.com/politics/2020/03/12/trump-coronavirus-timeline/

In March, Trump began to take the virus more seriously, after not only being neutral about the virus but actively trying to minimize it. If only we had a president who believed in science and was capable of being affected by something besides whether it will make him look good or bad (like protecting American lives). One consequence of all this is that the United States lagged behind other countries in testing capability for the virus, which was a key part to managing it.

Canada was hardly the most prepared for the disease compared with countries like South Korea or Singapore. But, compared with the United States, it was a model of competence. I remember reading that at some point Canada had tested almost as many people as had been tested in the USA, although Canada has one-tenth of its population. Wow.

Testing in the United States has finally caught up, but I shudder when I think about the damage done because Trump downplayed the situation for months. Then, most offensively but predictably, he claimed he'd taken the virus seriously all along. He rated himself a ten out of ten for his performance, and took "no responsibility" for anything that went wrong. Of course not. As I pointed out, he's too fragile a person psychologically to take responsibility for anything. In his own vernacular, he is "too weak."

The brilliant comedian and commentator Jon Stewart had this to say: "I've never seen anybody who can say in the same breath, as the president does, 'I am in charge, only I can fix this, and I take no responsibility.' You cannot process that."[47]

But I think this can be processed, actually. Not in a logical way, but when viewed through the prism of Trump's narcissism, it does make sense. If the goal is to prop up low self-esteem, which is part of narcissism, Trump's statements can be understood. If he's the only one in charge, if only he can fix this, then he has a special ability no one else has. That would be a way to inflate a psyche. And if anything goes wrong, he's not responsible for any failures, and he cannot be held accountable,

---

47 - https://www.nytimes.com/interactive/2020/06/15/magazine/jon-stewart-interview.html

preserving his self-image. If the goal is Trump's self-esteem, and not an honest appraisal of his role in things, it makes perfect sense.

The cultural differences between Canada and the United States were on full display during this crisis. The coronavirus acted like a "stress test," demonstrating America's fraying core and illuminating its partisan divide (as if it needed more illumination).

Trump largely withdrew from leading on the crisis, leaving it to the states to try to outbid each other to get supplies to manage the crisis. By contrast, in Canada, conservatives and liberals worked together, seamlessly, to combat the pandemic. Even the populist conservative premier of Ontario, Doug Ford, (whom liberal Torontonians despise) received moral support from Trudeau's deputy prime minister, Chrystia Freeland, who insisted she felt the same positive way toward Ford. But, in the United States, as I write this, even the wearing of masks has become another example of a partisan divide, where blue states advocate them, and in red states far fewer people wear them and instead tend to view the practice as a blue-state eccentricity.

Want more? Texas Republican Louie Gohmert suggested he might have been infected with Covid from *wearing* a mask. Really.[48]

In April, 2020, like everyone else, although I was scared of the coronavirus, I felt better, safer, because I was in Canada. It was the first concrete example of my decision to move to Canada because I felt it was a safer and saner place paying off.

And yet, I still am from New York. And that's of the utmost importance. As for many people in New York, this situation hit very close to home for me. My sister stopped contacting me for a few days. She can get like that sometimes, so I didn't get too bent out of shape because of it. Until she texted me that she hadn't been in touch because she was very sick.

My sister is one of my favorite people in the world (of course she can get on my nerves sometimes too). She and I became confidants

---

48 - https://www.rollingstone.com/culture/

because we supported each other through our shitty childhoods. She has the best heart of any person I've ever known. I'm not exaggerating.

My sister was coughing and had a lot of trouble breathing. She tried to get a coronavirus test, but when she called the designated phone number, she was put on hold for three hours, and then they hung up on her. It wasn't possible to get tested. Finally she was hospitalized in Queens, where she lives, for about a week. She heard the chaplains come to administer last rites for patients across the hall from her hospital room. She said the cafeteria in Booth Memorial Hospital in Queens had been transformed into a makeshift bed area, like something out of the old *M*A*S*H* TV show. I really thought she might die.

She very slowly recovered. At first she could hardly move but, after a while, she was able to walk a few blocks. She's almost fully recovered by now. Thank God. But she's traumatized by the experience.

My friend Gary in New York City is a psychotherapist and his partner is a psychologist. Correction: was a psychologist. They would have me over for dinner. Gary's partner is now dead from the coronavirus. As is a former student of mine in New York. As is my friend Bill's father, also from Covid-19. All dead.

As the months dragged on, the separation from my son became more and more of a horror to me. The border was closed in March and the timing of its reopening remains uncertain. For the first month or so it wasn't so bad to only see my son on FaceTime; bad, but not so bad. I was focused on writing this book. And on worrying that my sister would die.

But I began to experience feelings of desperation. I just needed to be in the physical presence of my son. To be honest, I've never been one of those parents who has to be with their children every day or they feel terrible. But I felt sick in a way I've never felt before. It was a deep yearning, as if my body had been hollowed out, leaving a deep cavity. All the FaceTime in the world couldn't fill this hole, and it grew larger each day. I felt like I was breaking apart inside. Sometimes I wanted to just cry.

I already felt bad about moving to a new country, away from Jordan. That's why I limited myself to being in Toronto, a one-hour flight away. The plan was to spend every other weekend with him. I never could have predicted a worldwide pandemic and a closed border with the United States going on for months.

But here I was. For better, and for worse.

In July 2020, I began to plan to have my son visit me in Canada, because Justin Trudeau announced that close family members could visit Canadian citizens or permanent residents in Canada, after quarantining there for two weeks. I called the Toronto Covid hotline for clarification on what I'd have to do to quarantine with my son in Toronto. The woman from the hotline was very nice and informative.

She told me I should put my son in a separate room and close the door. I could leave a tray of food for him outside his door for his meals. After two weeks, we could interact.

"Kind of defeats the purpose of having my son visit me, don't you think?" I asked her.

She paused, and thought some more. She then said, "You could, I guess, wear a mask all the time indoors, and your son would wear a mask all the time indoors, and you always remain six feet apart."

This wasn't particularly helpful for my need to be reunited with my only child after five months.

And then she had an epiphany. "Why don't you go visit him in the United States? They have a different culture there."

She was right. And so I went to New York, where I was free to be with my son. More opportunity.

I finally flew back to New York to see my son, other family, and friends in July. It was the first time, except for college, when I'd been away for more than a few weeks. It had been five months. I hadn't expected to feel what I felt. I was glad to be home. I didn't want to live there again, but I was happy to be home.

New York was different than I'd remembered it. It seemed a bit more like, well, Toronto. It was far less crowded. New York City is always less crowded in the summer as the wealthier people spend their time in their summer homes, in places such as the Hamptons. But Covid had really emptied out the city, leaving it with the energy and crowd density of ... Toronto. It was also somewhat cleaner. It was actually more pleasant. The worst of the pandemic was in the past (at least at this point), and most people were wearing masks. In fact, while most people wore them in Toronto, my guess is an even greater percentage were wearing them in New York.

I took a taxi from LaGuardia airport. As the driver pulled up to the building to drop me off, he asked me if I was paying cash or credit. I had no American money on me, and I said "credit." He replied that he wanted me to give him a tip in cash. This was new for me (I have since learned that while I was in Toronto, New York City mayor Bill de Blasio has implemented all these fees on yellow taxis, and drivers are asking for cash tips, among other countermeasures). I said I had no cash, and he insisted on driving me to the ATM so I could withdraw cash for his tip. I'd just come from my flight and I was tired, so I said no. Again he forcefully requested I do this and again, more firmly, I said no. While we were going back and forth with this unpleasant conversation, he was blocking traffic. The car behind us started honking and the driver of that car yelled out, "Move your fuckin' car, asshole!"

I smiled. I was home, back among my people.

***

I once had a client from Hong Kong, who told me the word for "risk" in his language is made up of the combination of the words "danger" and "opportunity." I think that's great.

Recognizing I'm speaking in vast overgeneralizations, Canada plays it safer, and the United States takes on more danger. Opportunity, beginning with the ability to have the freedom of being your own country, has been in many ways greater in the United States than in Canada. However, the danger has been greater as well in many ways.

These days, (as of July 2020, anyway) these cultural patterns are working against the United States. The United States has four percent of the world's population, but more than 25 percent of the world's coronavirus cases.[49] Canada has about one-third the rate of infection per capita as the United States.[50]

Trump both personifies and exacerbates these differences. No matter what, things would almost definitely be worse in the United States given the cultural differences between the two countries, in terms of Canada's emphasis on orderliness and America's emphasis on freedom. But Trump, with his awful decisions stemming from his personality dysfunction, exacerbated these differences. It just didn't have to be nearly this bad. But it was, and is, this bad. And this makes me very sad.

---

49 - https://www.fox10phoenix.com/news/
us-has-4-of-the-worlds-population-but-more-than-25-of-global-coronavirus-cases

50 - https://www.washingtonpost.com/world/the_americas/coronavirus-canada-united-states/2020/07/1
4/0686330a-c14c-11ea-b4f6-cb39cd8940fb_story.html

10
2020 and Beyond

I began this book by citing examples of how people in my liberal New York City bubble made all kinds of statements about how the Trump phenomenon wouldn't become a serious problem. Things like how he'd never be elected, or how the Mueller report would "get him," or how he'd be impeached and removed from office. All these statements were proved to be wrong.

Now, at the time of this writing (August 2020), it increasingly looks likely that Trump will lose the 2020 election. I don't have a crystal ball, but it does seem most probable that he'll indeed lose to Joe Biden. But if there's one thing we all learned from that 2016 election, it's that anything can happen.

Throughout these last four years, some people have challenged my move to Canada, asking me if it won't turn out to have been unnecessary, even pointless, to become Canadian if Trump is defeated in the next election.

As I've stated at times throughout this book, I don't agree with this sentiment. I very much hope Donald Trump will lose the upcoming election. I think things will be much better if he's defeated compared with how things would be if, God forbid, he wins.

However, I'm also convinced everything will NOT turn out to be fine if Trump is defeated.

For one thing, the 40 percent of the American people that supported Trump throughout these last four years will still be there. They won't suddenly disappear if Trump loses. This has serious implications. First of all, it's quite possible that in the future, post-Biden, someone even worse than Trump could be elected president of the United States. Trump's emotional pathology and intellectual limitations, in my view, limit his ability to be quite as dangerous as he could've been if he was more competent in his destructiveness. Don't get me wrong; he's still very dangerous; that's why I moved to Canada. But the American people could elect someone even more dangerous in the future. This is one reason things will not "be okay" even if Trump is defeated.

As a result of this, it's clear to me many Americans don't really value democracy, but are drawn to authoritarian candidates like Trump: a man who consistently lies and blatantly makes judgments based on what's good for him and not the country. It's also clear to me that many Americans will vote out of resentment toward "the elites," even if it goes against their economic interests, simply because it makes them feel better about them-selves, and it's a way for them to express their feelings of resentment. In other countries throughout time, people in democracies have made very poor choices for these same reasons. The United States is not immune to such a pattern; indeed, it's dangerously flirting with this pattern right now.

No, things will not "be okay" if Trump is defeated.

Another concern, which has been widely expressed, is that Trump may not accept the results of the election if he's defeated. In fact, he's already explicitly said so. He has claimed, without evidence, the only reason he didn't win the popular vote in 2016 was because of voter fraud. There's good reason to believe he won't respect the results of the 2020 election if he loses. He will, quite likely, challenge the legitimacy of the results, stirring up controversy and confusion and undermining even further the democratic foundations of the United States. Remember, this is a man who led the "birther" movement, without evidence, to question the legitimacy of Barack Obama. Then finally, after years, he renounced it, blaming the movement on Hillary Clinton.

It's all so insane. But the danger is real.

Too many of the American people support this man, in spite of everything. Therefore, I have serious doubts about their judgment.

There's a story, which may or may not be true, about a woman who was waiting outside the building where the founders were creating the American Constitution. To paraphrase, this woman saw Benjamin Franklin leave the building, and asked him, "Well, Dr. Franklin, what shall it be? Will we have a republic, or a monarchy?" And Franklin replied: "A republic, if you can keep it."

Well, I honestly don't know if the American people can keep it. Too many of them aren't meeting their responsibilities as citizens of a republic. In my opinion, these responsibilities include not voting for people who are serial liars. These responsibilities include voting for individuals who are reasonably emotionally healthy, and who make decisions based on what's best for the people of the country, not on propping up their damaged self-esteem.

I remain American, and will try hard to do my part to repair the United States from the injuries the American people inflicted upon themselves in the 2016 election. I'll work hard to defeat Donald Trump. The United States was founded upon some great principles and has achieved great things. I hope more Americans regain their good judgment and renew their commitment to these principles. The potential for American greatness remains enormous, but so is the potential for danger.

Although it was a brutal process, I successfully became Canadian because Donald Trump was elected the President of the United States. I want to thank you for accompanying me as I described this journey to you.

And as a Canadian, I am now part of a country that – while far from perfect – is more sensible, more stable, less volatile, in some ways kinder, and definitely safer than the United States is now.

I now belong to these two countries. I worked very hard for it. I'm grateful for this opportunity.

About the Author

Stephen Shainbart is a psychologist in private practice in New York City and Toronto. He received his Bachelor of Science from Cornell University and has a Ph.D. in clinical psychology from Fordham University. He has taught and supervised many mental health professionals in both the theory and practice of psychotherapy. He is also a life-long New York Mets fan who has now adopted the Blue Jays as his second team.